HINGE HOURS
for CHRISTMAS

Psalms, Canticles, and Christmas Readings

a meditation rendering by
Stephen Joseph Wolf

idjc press

www.idjc.org

THE MORNING BEGINNING:

PSALM 51:17

✝ Lord, open my lips
and my mouth will declare your praise.

Glory to the Father and to the Son and to the Holy Spirit
As it was in the beginning, is now, and will be forever. Amen.

Christmas until the Epiphany: Christ is born for all;
come and adore him.

Epiphany through the Baptism of the Lord: Christ has appeared;
come and adore him.

INVITATION PSALM

PSALM 67

May God be gracious to us and bless us,
may God's faces shine upon us.
How else can your ways be known on the earth
and your salvation among all the nations?

May the peoples praise you, God,
may the peoples praise you, all of them.

May the nations be glad and sing for joy
for you rule the peoples
and guide nations of the earth into justice.

May the peoples praise you, God,
may the peoples praise you, all of them.

The land will yield her harvest, God will bless us,
and all the ends of the earth will revere our God.

Glory to the Father and to the Son and to the Holy Spirit
As it was in the beginning, is now, and will be forever. Amen.

← The antiphon is traditionally repeated.

THE EVENING BEGINNING: PSALM 70:2

✢ God, come to my assistance;
make haste, Adonai, to help me!

Glory to the Father and to the Son and to the Holy Spirit
As it was in the beginning, is now, and will be forever. Amen.

Hinge Hours for Christmas
Copyright © 2014
Stephen Joseph Wolf
All rights reserved. No part of this book may be
copied or reproduced in any form or by any means,
except for the inclusion of brief quotations in a review,
without the written permission of the publisher.

For the holy name YHVH or Yahweh,
the Hebrew word for "my Lord" (*Adonai*) is used,
pronounced ***ah-duh-nigh'***.
See page 262
for the other choices made in this meditation rendering.

Icons are by Stephen Joseph Wolf

ISBN 978-1-937081-31-7

printed and distributed by Ingram Books
published by idjc press
www.idjc.org

THE FOUR-WEEK REPEATING CYCLE FOR MORNING & EVENING

Hinge Hours for Ordinary Time	ISBN 978-1-937081-16-4
Hinge Hours for Advent	ISBN 978-1-937081-17-1
Hinge Hours for Christmas	ISBN 978-1-937081-31-7
Hinge Hours for Lent and Easter	ISBN 978-1-937081-30-0

Hinge Hour Singer, the songs used in the Hinge Hours prayer books

ONCE-A-DAY PRAYER THROUGH THE LITURGICAL YEAR

A Simple Family Breviary, following the psalms of Saint Francis of Assisi

ONE-WEEK REPEATING CYCLE FOR MORNING & EVENING

In Health & In Healing, encouraging passages for the ill & depressed
Work Hours, drawn from the daytime hours, for morning & afternoon
Best of the Psalter, drawn from commons of the saints, includes IHIH & WH

SPECIAL PURPOSE PRAYER

Gospel of Life Prayer Cycle, a prayer for peace and justice study groups
Gone Before Us, praying for the dead

Hinge Hours for Christmas

Invitation Psalm			3

The Octave of Christmas:	VIGILS	MORNINGS	EVENINGS
Christmas Day	7	15	26
Holy Family	34	40	46
Dec. 26 - Stephen, Martyr		54	58
Dec. 27 - John, Evangelist		62	65
Dec. 28 - Holy Innocents		69	74
Dec. 29 - Octave Day 5		78	81
Dec. 30 - Octave Day 6		85	89
Dec. 31 - Octave Day 7		94	
Jan. 1 - Theotokos	98	105	108

Weekdays between January 1 to Baptism of the Lord:

Mondays		114	125
Tuesdays		135	146
Wednesdays		154	164
Thursdays		171	181
Fridays		189	200
Saturdays		206	

Epiphany of the Lord	217	225	230
Baptism of the Lord	238	246	251

Christmas in the Calendar	260
Daily Gospel Readings for Christmas	261
Acknowledgements	262
Psalms of the Christmas Season	265
Canticles and Readings	266
Songs for Christmas	267
Morning Prayer Canticle of Zechariah	268
Morning Prayer Petitions (for Consecration of the Day)	269
Evening Prayer Canticle of Mary	270
Evening Prayer Intercessions	271

A PRAYER BEFORE A MANGER SCENE

Loving Creator God,
let my gaze on this humble scene
of the fragrant glory of the Incarnation
be heard in my heart
as the touch of the gospel
and a taste of true peace.
Amen.

CHRISTMAS EVE
Evening Vigil Of Christmas

An-gels we have heard on high
Sweet-ly sing-ing o'er the plains,
And the moun-tains in re-ply
E-cho back their joy-ous strains.
Glo__-ri-a in ex-cel-sis De-o!
Glo__-ri-a in ex-cel-sis De-o!

Shep-herds why this ju-bi-lee?
Why your joy-ous strains pro-long?
Say what may the ti-dings be
Which in-spire your heav'n-ly song.
Glo__-ri-a in ex-cel-sis De-o!
Glo__-ri-a in ex-cel-sis De-o!

Come to Beth-le-hem and see
Him whose birth the an-gels sing;
Come, a-dore on bend-ed knee
Christ the Lord the new-born King.
Glo__-ri-a in ex-cel-sis De-o!
Glo__-ri-a in ex-cel-sis De-o!

Text: French, 18th Century;
translated from <i>Crown of Jesus Music, II,</i> London, 1862.
Music: 77 77 GLORIA with refrain, traditional French carol

PSALM 4

Antiphon   The Savior will be born of the Virgin Mary.

When I call, answer me, righteous God.
From distress you give me relief.
Be merciful to me and hear my prayer.

Until when, human, will you shame the glory?
Until when will you love delusion and seek the lie?
Know that Adonai set apart the faithful for Adonai
and will hear when I call.

When you are angry, do not sin.
Search in your heart and on your bed, and be silent.
Offer sacrifices of goodness, and trust Adonai.

Many are asking,
"Who can show us good?
  Adonai, let the light of your faces shine upon us."

You put joy in my heart, more joy
than when their grain and new wine abound.
In the peace of God's face I will lie down and sleep,
for you alone, Adonai, make me dwell in safety.

Traditional Doxology

*Glory to the Father and to the Son
and to the Holy Spirit,
As it was in the beginning, is now,
and will be forever. Amen.*

The antiphon is traditionally repeated: The Savior will be born
of the Virgin Mary.

PSALM 113

Antiphon   The King who is our peace comes in splendor;
the whole world longs to see him.

Hallelujah! Praise Adonai!
Praise, you who serve Adonai!
Praise the name Adonai!

Let Adonai be praised by name
from now and to forevermore.
From the rising of the sun to its setting
praised be the name Adonai.

Exalted over all the nations is Adonai,
the glory above the heavens.
Who is like our God Adonai,
sitting enthroned on high,
leaning to look down
on the heavens and the earth?

The One who raises the poor from dust
and lifts up the needy from ash heaps
to sit with princes, the princes of the people,
who settles the barren woman in a home,
a happy mother of children.

Hallelujah! Praise Adonai!

Glory…

Antiphon   The King who is our peace comes in splendor;
the whole world longs to see him.

PSALM 147:12-20

Antiphon

He sends forth his word to the earth,
and his command
spreads swiftly through the land.

Extol Adonai, Jerusalem!
Zion, now give praise!

Your God strengthens the bars of your gates,
blesses your peoples within you,
grants peace to your border,
and satisfies you with finest of wheat.

Your God sends a command to the earth,
and in swiftness runs a word,
spreading snow like the wool
and scattering frost like the ash.

Hail is hurled like pebbles;
who can stand before the icy blast?
The word of the Lord is sent, and they melt;
wind stirs up and the waters flow.

The word of the Lord is revealed to Jacob,
decrees and laws of the Lord to Israel.
Not for any nation did the Lord do this;
they do not know these laws.
Hallelujah! Praise Adonai!

Glory...

Antiphon

He sends forth his word to the earth,
and his command
spreads swiftly through the land.

PHILIPPIANS 2:6-11

Antiphon

The eternal Word,
born of the Father before time began,
today emptied himself for our sake
and became human.

Christ Jesus, subsisting in the form of God,
did not deem equality with God something to grab,
but emptied himself, taking the form of a slave,
becoming in human likeness.

And being found in human fashion,
he humbled himself,
becoming obedient until death,
and death on a cross.

And so God highly exalted him,
and gave to him the name above every name,
that in the name of Jesus every knee should bend,
of heavenly beings and earthly beings,
and beings under the earth;

And every tongue acknowledge
to the glory of God the Father
that Jesus Christ is Lord.

Glory…

Antiphon

The eternal Word,
born of the Father before time began,
today emptied himself for our sake
and became human.

READING, Christmas Vigil **GALATIANS 4:3-7**

And so when we were in youth,
having been enslaved
under the elements of the cosmos,
when the fullness of time had come,
God sent forth God's own Son,
becoming of a woman, becoming under the law,
that he might redeem those under the law,
that we might receive the full adoption
as sons and daughters.
And because we are sons and daughters,
God sent forth the Spirit of the Son of God
into our hearts, crying, "Abba, Father."
So you are no more a slave, but a son, a daughter,
and if a son or daughter through God also an heir.

RESPONSORY

    Today you will know
        ...*the Lord is coming.*
    And in the morning you will see his glory...

GOSPEL READING **LUKE 2:1-20**

Antiphon   As with the morning sun rising,
    see the King of kings coming forth
    from the Father as a bridegroom
    shining from the wedding chamber.

VIGIL OF CHRISTMAS

LUKE 2:1-20

Now it came to pass in those days a decree went out
from Caesar Augustus calling all the inhabited earth
to be enrolled. This first enrollment
was when Quirinius was governing Syria.
And all went to be enrolled, each man to his city.
So Joseph went up also from Galilee out of the city of
Nazareth to Judea to a city of David called Bethlehem,
because he was out of the house and family of David,
to be enrolled with Mary his betrothed,
who was pregnant.
And it came to pass while they were there
the days for her to give birth were fulfilled,
and she gave birth to her firstborn son,
and she swaddled him and laid him in a manger,
because there was no room for them in the inn.
The shepherds there were in the same country
living in the fields
and keeping guard in the night over their flock.
And an angel of the Lord came upon them
and the glory of the Lord shone around them,
and they feared exceedingly.
And the angel said to them,
"Fear not, for behold I announce to you a great joy,
which will be to all the people,
because born to you today is a Savior,
who is Christ the Lord, in a city of David.
And this to you a sign: you will find a baby having been
swaddled and lying in a manger."

LUKE 2:1-20, continued

And suddenly there was with the angel a multitude
of a heavenly host praising God and saying,
"Glory to God in the highest
and on earth peace among humans of goodwill."
And it came to pass when the angels went away from
them to heaven, the shepherds said to one another,
"Let us go then to Bethlehem and see this thing having
happened which the Lord has made known to us."
And they came in haste and found both Mary and Joseph,
and the baby lying in the manger.
And seeing they made it known
about the word spoken to them about this child.
And all those hearing marvelled about the things
spoken to them by the shepherds.
But Mary kept all these things, pondering in her heart.
And the shepherds returned glorifying and praising God
at all they heard and saw as was spoken to them.

Antiphon

As with the morning sun rising,
see the King of kings coming forth
from the Father as a bridegroom
shining from the wedding chamber.

EVENING PRAYER INTERCESSIONS AND CLOSING PRAYER, see page 271.

CHRISTMAS DAY - December 25
MORNING

O come, all ye faith-ful, joy-ful and tri-um-phant,
O come ye, O come/ ye, to Beth\-le-hem.
Come and be-hold him, born the King of an\-gels;

Refrain *O come, let us a-dore him, O come let us a-dore him,*
O come, let us a-dore him / , Christ \ the Lord.

Sing, choirs of an-gels, sing in ex-ul-ta-tion;
O sing, all ye cit-i-zens of heav'n\ a-bove!
Glo-ry to God, all glo-ry in the high\-est;

Refrain *O come, let us a-dore him, O come let us a-dore him,*
O come, let us a-dore him / , Christ \ the Lord.

Yea, Lord, we greet thee, born this hap-py morn-ing;
O Je-sus, to thee/ be/ glo\-ry giv'n;
Word of the Fa-ther, now in flesh ap-pear\-ing.

Refrain *O come, let us a-dore him, O come let us a-dore him,*
O come, let us a-dore him / , Christ \ the Lord.

Text: John f. Wade, 1743; translated by Frederick Oakeley, 1841
Music: ADESTE FIDELES, attributed variously to
John Wade, John Reading, or Simon Portogallo

PSALM 63:1-8

Christmas Day	Tell us, shepherds, what have you seen?
& Octave	Who has appeared to you?
weekdays	We have seen a newborn infant
Dec. 29-31	and a choir of angels praising the Lord,
except:	alleluia.

Holy Family
: The parents of Jesus went each year to Jerusalem for the solemn feast of Passover.

Dec. 26, Stephen
: My soul has held fast to you, my God; for your sake I suffered death by stoning.

Dec. 27, John
: John, the apostle and evangelist, a virgin chosen by the Lord, was loved by the Lord above others.

Dec. 28, Innocents
: Clothed in white robes, they will walk with me, says the Lord, for they are worthy.

Jan. 1, *Theotokos*
: The Virgin has given birth to the Savior: a flower has sprung from Jesse's stock and a star has risen from Jacob. O God, we praise you.

Epiphany (Sunday or Jan. 6)
: The wise ones opened their treasures and offered to the Lord gifts of gold, frankincense and myrrh, alleluia.

Baptism of the Lord
: The soldier baptizes his king, the servant his Lord, John his Savior; the waters of the Jordan tremble, a dove hovers as a sign of witness, and the voice of the Father is heard: You are my Son.

PSALM 63:1-8

God, you are my God; you I earnestly seek.
My soul, she thirsts for you,
my body, he longs for you,
as in a land with no water, dry and weary.

So in the sanctuary I saw you,
beheld you in your power and glory.
Your love is better than life itself;
my lips will glorify you.

So I will praise you in all the ways I am alive;
in your name I will lift up my hands.
As with fatness and richness,
my soul will be satisfied;
with singing lips my mouth will sing praise.

When I remember you on my bed,
through night watches I think of you,
you who are my help;
then in the shadow of your wings I sing.
My very self stays close to you;
your right hand upholds me.

Glory...

Repeat antiphon.

DANIEL 3:57-90

Christmas Day & weekdays Dec. 29-31 except:	The angel said to the shepherds: I proclaim to you a great joy; today the Savior of the world is born for you, alleluia.
Holy Family	The child grew in wisdom and strength, and the favor of God was upon him.
Dec. 26, Stephen	Stephen saw the heavens open and entered in. Happy the one to whom the heavens opened.
Dec. 27, John	To the virgin John, Christ, dying on the cross, entrusted his virgin mother.
Dec. 28, Innocents	These children cry out their praises to the Lord; by their death they have proclaimed what they could not preach with their infant voices.
Jan. 1, *Theotokos*	Mary has given birth to our Savior. John the Baptist saw him and cried out: This is the Lamb of God, who takes away the sins of the world, alleluia.
Epiphany (Sunday or Jan. 6)	Mighty seas and rivers, bless the Lord; springs of water, sing praise, alleluia.
Baptism of the Lord	Springs of water were made holy as Christ revealed his glory to the world. Draw water from the fountain of the Savior, for Christ our God has hallowed all creation.

DANIEL 3:57-90

Bless the Lord, all you works of the Lord,
exalt and sing praise to forever.
Angels of the Lord, bless the Lord,
You heavens, bless the Lord,
All you waters above the heavens, bless the Lord,
All you powers, bless the Lord,
Sun and moon, bless the Lord,
Stars of heaven, bless the Lord.

All you rain and dew, bless the Lord,
All you winds, bless the Lord,
You fire and heat, bless the Lord,
You ice and cold, bless the Lord,
You dews and falling snows, bless the Lord,
You snows and frosts, bless the Lord,
You nights and days, bless the Lord,
You light and darkness, bless the Lord,
You lightning and clouds, bless the Lord.

Let the earth bless the Lord,
exalt and sing praise to forever.
You mountains and hills, bless the Lord,
All things growing in the ground, bless the Lord,
You seas and rivers, bless the Lord,
You springs and rain, bless the Lord,
You sea monsters and all swimmers, bless the Lord,
All you birds of the air, bless the Lord,
All you wild beasts and cattle, bless the Lord,
You sons and daughters, bless the Lord.

DANIEL 3:57-90, continued

O Israel, bless the Lord,
exalt and sing praise to forever.
You priests of the Lord, bless the Lord,
You servants of the Lord, bless the Lord,
You spirits and souls of the just, bless the Lord,
You holy and humble in heart, bless the Lord,
Hananiah, Azariah, and Mishael, bless the Lord,
exalt and sing praise to forever...

Give thanks to the Lord, who is good,
whose mercy endures to forever.
Bless the God of "gods"
all you who worship the Lord;
sing praise and give thanks to the One God
whose mercy endures to forever.

CHRISTMAS DAY - DEC 25 MORNING

Christmas Day
& weekdays
Dec. 29-31
except:

The angel said to the shepherds:
I proclaim to you a great joy;
today the Savior of the world is born for you,
alleluia.

Holy Family

The child grew in wisdom and strength,
and the favor of God was upon him.

Dec. 26, Stephen

Stephen saw the heavens open and entered in.
Happy the one to whom the heavens opened.

Dec. 27, John

To the virgin John, Christ, dying on the cross,
entrusted his virgin mother.

Dec. 28, Innocents

These children cry out their praises to the Lord;
by their death they have proclaimed what they
could not preach with their infant voices.

Jan. 1, Theotokos

Mary has given birth to our Savior.
John the Baptist saw him and cried out:
This is the Lamb of God,
who takes away the sins of the world,
alleluia.

Epiphany
(Sunday or Jan. 6)

Mighty seas and rivers, bless the Lord;
springs of water, sing praise,
alleluia.

Baptism
of the Lord

Springs of water were made holy
as Christ revealed his glory to the world.
Draw water from the fountain of the Savior,
for Christ our God has hallowed all creation.

PSALM 149:1-6,9c

Christmas Day
& weekdays
Dec. 29-31
except:

A little child is born for us today;
little and yet called the mighty God,
alleluia.

Holy Family

His father and mother were full of wonder
at what was said about their child.

Dec. 26, Stephen

Behold, I see the heavens open, and Jesus
standing at the right hand of the almighty God.

Dec. 27, John

The disciple whom Jesus loved cried out:
It is the Lord, alleluia.

Dec. 28, Innocents

From the mouths of children
and babies at the breast
you have found praise to foil enmity.

Jan. 1, *Theotokos*

Mary has given birth to a King whose name is
everlasting; hers the joy of motherhood, hers the
virgin's glory. Never was the like seen before;
never shall it be seen again, alleluia.

Epiphany
(Sunday or
Jan. 6)

Jerusalem, your light has come;
the glory of the Lord dawns upon you.
Human beings of every race shall walk
in the splendor of your sunrise, alleluia.

Baptism
of the Lord

You burned away human guilt by fire and
the Holy Spirit. We give praise to you,
our God and Redeemer.

CHRISTMAS DAY - DEC 25 MORNING

PSALM 149:1-6,9c

Hallelujah! Praise Adonai!

Sing to Adonai a new song,
praise in the assembly of saints.
Let Israel rejoice in their Maker,
let the people of Zion be glad in their King.

Let them praise the name
with dance, tambourine and harp.
Let them make music for Adonai
who delights in Adonai's people.

Adonai crowns humble ones with salvation.
Let the saints rejoice in honor,
Let them sing for joy on their beds...

Hallelujah! Praise Adonai!

Glory...

Repeat antiphon.

READING

December 25	*to page* 24
Holy Family Sunday	*to page* 43
December 26	*to page* 56
December 27	*to page* 64
December 28	*to page* 72
December 29	*to page* 80
December 30	*to page* 88
December 31	*to page* 97
January 1	*to page* 107
Epiphany	*to page* 228
Baptism of the Lord	*to page* 249

READING, Christmas Morning, December 25 **HEBREWS 1:1-4**

Of old, having spoken to the ancestors by the prophets
often and in many ways, in these last days
God spoke to us in a Son,
appointed as heir of all things,
and indeed through whom God made the eons.
He is the radiance of the glory,
the representation of the reality,
and the bearer of all things
by the word of the power of God,
and having made a cleansing of sins,
he has sat at the right hand of the greatness on high.
By so much, he has inherited the more excellent name,
better even than the angels'.

RESPONSORY

The Lord has made known...
...alleluia, alleluia.

His saving power.

GOSPEL READING **JOHN 1:1-18**

Antiphon   Glory to God in the highest
and on earth peace
to people of good will, alleluia.

In the beginning was the Word and the Word was with God, and the Word was God. This one was in the beginning with God. Through him all things became, and without him not one thing which has become became.

In him was life, and the life (*zoe*) was the light (*phos*)
of all humanity; and the light shines in the night,
and the night did not overtake it.
There came a man, sent from God; his name was John.
This man came for witness, that he might witness
about the light, that all might believe through him.
He was not that light, but that he might witness
about the light. The true light, which enlightens
every human, was coming into the world.
He was in the world, and the world became through him,
and the world did not know him. He came to his own,
and his own did not receive him. But as many as did
he gave them the right to become children of God, to the
ones believing in his name, who were born not by blood
nor by the will of flesh nor by human will, but of God.
And the Word became flesh and tented among us,
and we gazed on his glory, glory as of an only begotten
from a father, full of grace and truth. John witnesses
about him and has cried out saying: "This is he of whom
I said, 'The one coming after me, has become before me,
because before me, he was.'" Because of his fullness
we all received, and grace over grace;
because the law was given through Moses,
grace and truth came through Jesus Christ.
No one has ever seen God; God the only begotten,
being in the bosom of the Father, that one revealed him.

Repeat antiphon.

MORNING PRAYER PETITIONS AND CLOSING PRAYER, see page 269.

CHRISTMAS DAY - December 25
EVENING

Hark! the her-ald an-gels sing\,
"Glo-ry to the new-born King;
Peace on earth and mer-cy mild\,
God and sin-ners re-con-ciled!"
Joy-ful, all ye na-tions rise\,
Join the tri-umph of the skies\;
With th'an-gel-ic host pro-claim.
"Christ is/ born in Beth-le-hem!"

Refrain   **Hark!** the her-ald an-gels sing,
               "Glo-ry/ to the new-born King!"

Christ, by high-est heav'n a-dored\.
Christ, the ev-er-last-ing Lord,
Late in time be-hold him come\,
Off-spring of the vir-gin's womb.
Veiled in flesh the God-head see\,
Hail th'in-car-nate De-i-ty\!
Pleased as man with us to dwell
Je-sus/, our Em-man-u-el!

Refrain

Come, De-sire of na-tions, come\,
Fix in us your hum-ble home;
Oh, to all your-self im-part\,
Formed in each be-liev-ing heart!

Hail, the heav'n-ly Prince of Peace\!
Hail, the Sun of Right-eous-ness\!
Light and life to all he brings,
Ris-en with heal-ing in his wings.

Refrain

Text: see Luke 2:14; Charles Wesley, 1739
Music: 7777777777 MENDELSSOHN, Felix Mendelssohn, 1840

PSALM 47

Antiphon   Joseph and Mary were filled with wonder
at all that was said of the child.

All you nations, clap your hands!
Shout to God with cries of joy!
How awesome, Most High Adonai.

The great King over all the earth
subdued nations under us
and peoples under our feet,
and chose for us an inheritance,
the pride of Jacob the beloved.

God ascended with shouts of joy,
Adonai amid sound of trumpet.
Sing praises to God, sing praises.
Sing praises to our King, sing praises.

For God, King of all the earth, sing praises.
God reigns over the nations,
God sits on the holy throne.

PSALM 47, continued

Nobles of nations assemble,
the people of the God of Abraham.
God, shield of the earth, is greatly exalted.

Glory…

Antiphon Joseph and Mary were filled with wonder
at all that was said of the child.

*On the next three pages are
the Christmas Evening Prayer Psalms & Canticles
for December 25-30.*

PSALM 110:1-6a,7

Antiphon
You have been endowed from your birth
with princely gifts;
in eternal splendor,
before the dawn of light on earth,
I have begotten you.

Adonai said to my Lord:
"Sit at my right hand
 until I make enmity as a footstool for your feet."

A scepter of your might
Adonai will extend from Zion,
and rule in the midst of enmity!

Your troops are willing on the day of your battle.
In majesties of holiness from the womb of the dawn
to you is the dew of your youth.
Adonai swore and this mind will not change,
"You are a priest to forever
 in the order of Melchizedek."

The Lord is at your right hand
and will crush kings on the day of wrath,
will judge the nations…,
and will drink from a brook on the way
with head lifted up because of all this.

Glory…

Repeat antiphon.

PSALM 130

Antiphon   With the Lord is unfailing love;
            great is God's power to save.

From the depths I cry to you, Adonai.
Lord, hear my voice.
Let your ears be attentive to my cries for mercy.

If you kept a record of sins, Adonai,
Lord, who could stand?
But with you is the forgiveness,
and so you are revered in awe.

I wait, my soul waits for Adonai,
in whose word I put hope.
My soul waits for the Lord
more than watchers for the morning,
even watchers for the morning.

Put hope, Israel, in Adonai!
For unfailing love is from Adonai,
in whom is full redemption,
who will redeem Israel from all their sins.

Glory…

Antiphon   With the Lord is unfailing love;
            great is God's power to save.

COLOSSIANS 1:12-20

Antiphon

In the beginning, before time began,
the Word was God;
today he is born, the Savior of the world.

Give joyful thanks to the Father who made you fit
for your part of the lot of the saints in light,

who delivered us out of the authority of darkness
and transitioned us into the kingdom of the beloved Son,
in whom we have redemption, the forgiveness of our sins.

The Son is the image of the invisible God,
the firstborn of all creation.
In him all things were created,
in the heavens and on the earth,
the visible and the invisible,
whether thrones, lordships, rulers or authorities.

All things have been created through him and for him.
He is before all things,
and in him all things hold together.

He is the head of the body, the church,
and the beginning, the firstborn from the dead,
so that in all things he may hold the first place.

In him all the fullness was well pleased to dwell,
and through him reconciliation to himself of all things,
things on earth and things in the heavens,
making peace through the blood of his cross.

Glory...   Repeat antiphon.

READING

December 25	*below*
December 26	*to page* 61
December 27	*to page* 68
December 28	*to page* 77
December 29	*to page* 84
December 30	*to page* 93

READING, December 25 **1 JOHN 1:1-3**

What was from the beginning,
what we have heard,
what we have seen with our eyes,
what we have looked at and our hands have touched
concerning the Word of Life,
and the life has been shown,
we have seen and we bear witness
and we proclaim to you the life eternal,
which was with the Father and has been shown to us.
What we have seen and heard,
we proclaim also to you
that you also may have communion with us.
Indeed our communion is with the Father
and with the Son, Jesus Christ.

RESPONSORY Jn 1:14

The Word became flesh...
...*alleluia, alleluia.*
And dwelt among us...

CHRISTMAS DAY - DEC 25 EVENING 33

GOSPEL CANTICLE (**Canticle of Mary**) see page 270.

Antiphon
Christ the Lord is born;
the Savior has appeared.
Earth sings songs of angel choirs;
his friends today lift up their voice:
Glory to God in the highest,
alleluia.

EVENING PRAYER INTERCESSIONS AND CLOSING PRAYER, see page 271.

HOLY FAMILY
SUNDAY VIGIL (Saturday Evening)

If Christmas falls on a Sunday, Holy Family is on Dec. 30 and this Vigil is omitted.

An-gels we have heard on high
Sweet-ly sing-ing o'er the plains,
And the moun-tains in re-ply
E-cho back their joy-ous strains.
Glo_-ri-a in ex-cel-sis De-o! Glo_-ri-a in ex-cel-sis De-o

Shep-herds why this ju-bi-lee?
Why your joy-ous strains pro-long?
Say what may the ti-dings be
Which in-spire your heav'n-ly song.
Glo_-ri-a in ex-cel-sis De-o! Glo_-ri-a in ex-cel-sis De-o

Come to Beth-le-hem and see
Him whose birth the an-gels sing;
Come, a-dore on bend-ed knee
Christ the Lord the new-born King.
Glo_-ri-a in ex-cel-sis De-o! Glo_-ri-a in ex-cel-sis De-o

Text: French, 18th C.; translated from *Crown of Jesus Music, II,* London, 1862.
Music: 77 77 GLORIA with refrain, traditional French carol

PSALM 48

Antiphon   Mary treasured all these words
and pondered them in her heart.

PSALM 48

Great is Adonai, greatly being praised
in the city of our God, on the holy mountain,
beautiful loft, the joy of all the earth,

Mount Zion, the upmost heights,
sacred mountain, the city of the Great King.
God in the citadels is shown as a fortress when,
see, the kings join forces and advance together.

They saw, were astounded, and fled in terror;
trembling seized them, pain like a woman in labor.
By the east wind you destroyed ships of Tarshish;

just as we heard, so we saw in the city
of Adonai Sabaoth, in the city of our God.
God makes her secure to forever.

In your temple we meditate on your unfailing love.
Like your name, God, so your praise
goes to the ends of the earth;

your right hand is filled with justice.
Mount Zion rejoices because of your judgments;
the villages of Judah are glad.

Walk about Zion! Go around! Count her towers!
Consider at heart her ramparts! View her citadels!

So that you may tell to the next generation:
This God, our God, forever and ever
will guide us even to the end.

Glory…

Repeat antiphon.

PSALM 113

Antiphon   Jacob was father to Joseph, husband of Mary,
             who gave birth to Jesus called Christ.

Hallelujah! Praise Adonai!
Praise, you who serve Adonai!
Praise the name Adonai!

Let Adonai be praised by name
from now and to forevermore.
From the rising of the sun to its setting
praised be the name Adonai.

Exalted over all the nations is Adonai,
the glory above the heavens.
Who is like our God Adonai,
sitting enthroned on high,
leaning to look down
on the heavens and the earth?

The One who raises the poor from dust
and lifts up the needy from ash heaps
to sit with princes, the princes of the people,
who settles the barren woman in a home,
a happy mother of children.

Hallelujah! Praise Adonai!

Glory...

Antiphon   Jacob was father to Joseph, husband of Mary,
             who gave birth to Jesus called Christ.

PSALM 147:12-20

Antiphon
Joseph, son of David,
be not afraid to take Mary as your wife.

Extol Adonai, Jerusalem!
Zion, now give praise!

Your God strengthens the bars of your gates,
blesses your peoples within you,
grants peace to your border,
and satisfies you with finest of wheat.

Your God sends a command to the earth,
and in swiftness runs a word,
spreading snow like the wool
and scattering frost like the ash.

Hail is hurled like pebbles;
who can stand before the icy blast?
The word of the Lord is sent, and they melt;
wind stirs up and the waters flow.

The word of the Lord is revealed to Jacob,
decrees and laws of the Lord to Israel.
Not for any nation did the Lord do this;
they do not know these laws.
Hallelujah! Praise Adonai!

Glory…

Antiphon
Joseph, son of David,
be not afraid to take Mary as your wife.

EPHESIANS 1:3-10

Antiphon
>The shepherds went in haste
>and found Mary and Joseph,
>with the child cradled in a manger.

Blessed be the God and Father
of our Lord Jesus Christ,
who has blessed us in Christ
with every spiritual blessing in the heavens.

God chose us in Christ
before the foundation of the world,
to be holy and free of blemish before him.

In love, God gave us a destiny:
as sons are adopted, through Jesus Christ himself,
in accord with the good pleasure of God's will
to the praise of the glory of grace
by which we are favored as God's beloved.

In Christ we have the redemption
through his blood, the forgiveness of sins,
in accord with the riches of his grace
which he made abound to us.

In all wisdom and intelligence
the mystery of God's will is made known to us
in accord with God's good pleasure and purpose:

A stewardship of the fullness of time,
heading up all things in Christ,
the things in the heavens and the things on earth.

Glory...   Repeat antiphon.

READING **2 CORINTHIANS 8:9**

You know the grace of our Lord Jesus Christ,
that being rich
he impoverished himself for you
that by his poverty you might become rich.

RESPONSORY Jn 1:14

The Word became flesh...
...*alleluia, alleluia.*
And dwelt among us...

GOSPEL READING **MATTHEW 2:19-23**

Antiphon The child Jesus remained in Jerusalem
without his parents' knowledge;
thinking he was among the travelers
they looked among family and friends.

When Herod died,
behold an angel of the Lord appeared by a dream
to Joseph in Egypt saying,
"Rise, take the child and his mother,
and go into the land of Israel,
for the ones seeking the child's life have died."
So rising he took the child and his mother
and entered into the land of Israel.

LUKE 2:19-23, continued

But hearing that Archelaus was reigning over Judea
instead of his father Herod, he feared to go there,
and being warned by a dream
he departed into the parts of Galilee,
and coming dwelt in a city called Nazareth,
so that was fulfilled
what was spoken through the prophets,
A Nazarene he shall be called.

Antiphon The child Jesus remained in Jerusalem
without his parents' knowledge;
thinking he was among the travelers
they looked among family and friends.

EVENING PRAYER INTERCESSIONS AND CLOSING PRAYER, see page 271.

HOLY FAMILY
SUNDAY MORNING
Sunday in the Octave of Christmas, or Dec. 30

Ho-ly\ Jo-seph/, you sa-lut-ing
Here we\ meet, with/ hearts sin-cere;
Bless-ed\ Jos-eph/, all u-nite and
Call on\ you to/ hear our prayer.
Hap-py\ saint in hea-ven a-dor-ing
Je-sus\, Sa-vior of the\ race,
Hear your\ fost-er/ sons and daugh-ters,
May we\ find with/ you our place.

You who\ faith-ful/-ly at-tend-ed
Him whom\ heav'n and/ earth a-dore;
Who with\ ten-der/ care de-fend-ed
Mar-y\, Vir-gin/ ev-er pure.
May our\ trust-ing voic-es\ lift-ing
Move you\ for our souls to\ pray;
May your\ smile of/ peace des-cend-ing,
Be-ne\-dic-tions/ on us lay.

Through this\ life, give/ watch a-round us!
Thank our\ Lord for/ ev-'ry breath,
And, when\ part-ing/ fear sur-rounds us,
Guide us\ e-ven/ through our death.
Hap-py\ saint in hea-ven a-dor-ing
Je-sus\, Sa-vior of the\ race,
Hear your\ fost-er/ sons and daugh-ters,
May we\ find with/ you our place.

Text: anonymous, altered significantly
Music: 87 87 D, PLEADING SAVIOR, Joshua Leavitt, *Christian Lyre,* 1830
Popular melody for: *Sing of Mary, Pure and Lowly*

PSALM 24

Antiphon Come, let us worship Christ, the Son of God,
who was obedient to Mary and Joseph.

The earth and everything,
the world and all who are alive are to Adonai,
who founded the earth on the seas
and established the earth on the waters.

PSALM 24, continued

Who may ascend to the hill of Adonai?
And who may stand in the holy place?
The clean of hand and pure of heart
who do not lift the soul to an idol
and do not swear by falsehood
will receive the blessing from Adonai
and vindication from the God who saves.

Such is the generation of ones who seek,
who seek your faces, God of Jacob.

Lift up your heads, you gates;
be lifted up you ancient doors,
that the King of glory may come in.

Who is this King of glory?
Adonai, strong and mighty,
Adonai, mighty of battle.

Lift up your heads, you gates;
lift up, you ancient doors,
that the King of glory may come in.

Who is this King of glory?
Adonai Sabaoth is the King of glory.

Glory...

Antiphon — Come, let us worship Christ, the Son of God, who was obedient to Mary and Joseph.

Psalm 63, Daniel 3, and Psalm 149, go to **Christmas Morning** *, page* 16

CHRISTMAS - HOLY FAMILY SUNDAY MORNING

READING   **DEUTERONOMY 5:16**

Honor your father and your mother,
just as your God Adonai commanded you,
that your days may be long
and that it may go well with you
in the land that your God Adonai is giving you.

RESPONSORY   Luke 18:13, 22:69

Lord Jesus Christ, Son of the living God…
…*have mercy on us.*
You are seated at the right hand of the Father…

GOSPEL READING   **LUKE 2:22-40**

Antiphon   Lord, give us light
through the example of your family
and guide our feet into the peaceful way.

And when were completed the days of their cleansing
according to the law of Moses, they took him
up to Jerusalem to present him to the Lord,
as it has been written in the law of the Lord,
Every male opening a womb shall be called holy to the Lord,
and to give a sacrifice according to
the thing said in the law of the Lord,
a pair of turtledoves or two nestlings of doves.
And behold a man named Simeon was in Jerusalem,
and this man was just and devout,
expecting the consolation of Israel,
and the Spirit was Holy upon him.

It had been communicated to him by the Holy Spirit
he would not see death
before seeing the Christ of the Lord.
And he came by the Spirit into the temple
as the parents brought in the child Jesus for them
to keep the custom of the law concerning him, and
he received him in his arms and blessed God and said,
"Now, Master, you make free your slave
according to your word in peace;
my eyes have seen your salvation
which you have prepared
before the face of all the peoples,
a light for revelation to nations
and glory for your people Israel."
And his father and mother marvelled at the things
being said about him. And Simeon blessed them
and said to Mary his mother,
"Behold, this sign is set for the fall and rising again
of many in Israel, and a sign to be spoken against
so that thoughts of many hearts may be revealed,
and you yourself, a sword will go through your soul."
There also was Anna a prophetess,
a daughter of Phanuel of the tribe of Asher,
having advanced in many days, having
lived with a husband seven years from her virginity,
and she was a widow until age eighty-four,
who did not withdraw from the temple,
with fastings and serving petitions night and day.

And coming upon him at the very hour,
she gave thanks to God and spoke about him
to all those expecting redemption in Jerusalem.
And when they finished
all the things according to the law of the Lord,
they returned to Galilee to their city of Nazareth.
And the child grew and became strong,
being filled with wisdom,
and the grace of God was upon him.

Antiphon Lord, give us light
through the example of your family
and guide our feet into the peaceful way.

MORNING PRAYER PETITIONS AND CLOSING PRAYER, see page 269.

HOLY FAMILY
SUNDAY EVENING
Sunday in the Octave of Christmas, or Dec. 30

O ho-ly night, the stars are bright-ly shi-ning;
It is the night of the dear Sa-vior's birth!
Long lay the world in sin and err-or pi-ning,
Till he ap-peared and the soul felt its worth.
A thrill of hope, the wea-ry soul re-joic-es,
For yon-der breaks a new and glo-rious morn.
Fall on your knees, O hear the an-gel voi-ces!
O night\ div-ine, O\ night when Christ was born!
O night, O ho-ly night\\\\, O night div-ine!

Tru-ly he taught us to love one an-oth-er;
His law is love and his Gos-pel is peace.
Chains shall he break for the slave is our broth-er
And in his Name all op-pres-sion shall cease.
The King of kings lay thus in hum-ble man-ger,
In all our tri-als born to be our Friend!
He knows our need, to our weak-ness is no stran-ger.
Be-hold\ your King; the Son of Ma-ry and our God!
Give glo-ry to God: Fa-ther and Son and Spir-it blest!

Text: Placide Cappeau, 1847; translated from French by John S. Dwight, d. 1893, altered
Music: 11 10 11 10 11 10 11 10 10, Adolphe C. Adam, d. 1856
Said to have been the first music broadcast by radio.

PSALM 91

Antiphon
My own eyes have seen the salvation
which you have prepared
in the sight of every people.

One who dwells in the shelter of Elyon,
in the shadow of Shaddai, will find rest.
I will say of Adonai, my refuge, my fortress:
in my God do I trust.

Surely the Lord will save you
from fowler snare, from deadly pestilence.
With the feather of the Lord you will be covered,
and under those wings you will find refuge,
shield and rampart, the faithfulness of the Lord.

You will have no fear of terror at night
nor of arrows flying by day,
of pestilence stalking in the darkness,
nor of plague that destroys at midday.

A thousand may fall at your side,
and ten thousand at your right hand;
near to you they will not come.

Observe with your eyes, simply watch;
punishment of wicked ones you will see.
Make Adonai, who is my refuge,
make Elyon your dwelling.

PSALM 91, continued

Harm will not befall you,
nor will disaster come near your tent.
God's own Angels, the Lord will command
to guard you in all of your ways.

In their hands they will lift you up;
your foot will not strike against the stone.
Upon lion and cobra you will tread,
you will trample the great lion and serpent.

"Because you love me, I will rescue you,
 I will protect all who acknowledge my Name.
 You will call upon me and I will answer.
 I am with you in trouble;
 I will deliver you and honor you.

In length of days I will satisfy you,
and show you my salvation."

Glory…

Antiphon

My own eyes have seen the salvation
which you have prepared
in the sight of every people.

PSALM 122

Antiphon

After three days,
Jesus was found in the temple,
seated in the midst of the doctors,
listening to them and asking them questions.

I rejoiced with those saying to me,
"Let us go to Adonai's house."
Our feet stand in your gates, Jerusalem.

Jerusalem is built like a city
formed together, a compact.
There the tribes go up, the tribes of Adonai.

Make it in Israel a statute
to praise the name of Adonai,
for there the thrones stand for judgment,
thrones of the house of David.

Pray for the peace of Jerusalem!
May those who love you be secure.
May peace be within your walls,
security within your citadels.

For the sake of my sisters and brothers and friends
I will say, "Now, peace be within you."
For the sake of the house of our God Adonai
I will seek your prosperity.

Glory...

Repeat antiphon.

PSALM 127

Antiphon
>Jesus returned
>with Mary and Joseph to Nazareth;
>there he lived, obedient to them.

If Adonai does not build the house,
the builders labor in vanity.
If Adonai does not watch over the city,
the watcher stands guard in vain.

It is vanity to rise early or stay up late,
or to eat the bread of hard toil;
the Lord provides as the beloved get their sleep.
See, heritage of Adonai!

Sons are a reward, and daughters of the womb.
Like arrows in the hand of a warrior,
so are children of one's youth.

Blessed is the one whose quiver is full of them;
they will not be shamed
when they contend at the gate with enmity.

Glory…

Antiphon
>Jesus returned
>with Mary and Joseph to Nazareth;
>there he lived, obedient to them.

EPHESIANS 1:3-10

Antiphon Jesus grew in wisdom with the years
and was pleasing to God and human beings.

Blessed be the God and Father
of our Lord Jesus Christ,
who has blessed us in Christ
with every spiritual blessing in the heavens.

God chose us in Christ
before the foundation of the world,
to be holy and free of blemish before him.

In love, God gave us a destiny:
as sons are adopted, through Jesus Christ himself,
in accord with the good pleasure of God's will
to the praise of the glory of grace
by which we are favored as God's beloved.

In Christ we have the redemption
through his blood, the forgiveness of sins,
in accord with the riches of his grace
which he made abound to us.

In all wisdom and intelligence
the mystery of God's will is made known to us
in accord with God's good pleasure and purpose:

A stewardship of the fullness of time,
heading up all things in Christ,
the things in the heavens and the things on earth.

Glory...   Repeat antiphon.

READING   **PHILIPPIANS 2:6-7**

Christ Jesus, subsisting in the form of God,
did not deem equality with God something to grab,
but emptied himself, taking the form of a slave,
becoming in human likeness,
being found in human fashion.

RESPONSORY

He had to become like us in every way…
…to show the fullness of his mercy.
He was seen on earth and lived among men and women…

GOSPEL READING   **LUKE 2:41-52**

Antiphon   Son, why have you done this to us?
                   But did you not know
                   that I had to be in my Father's house?

And his parents went year by year to Jerusalem at the feast of the Passover. And when he became of twelve years, as they went up according to the custom of the feast, and fulfilling the days, when they returned the boy Jesus remained in Jerusalem, and his parents did not know this. But supposing him to be in the company, they went a day in the journey and sought him among their relatives and acquaintances, and not finding him returned to Jerusalem seeking him.

CHRISTMAS - HOLY FAMILY SUNDAY EVENING

And it came to pass
after three days they found him sitting in the temple in
the midst of the teachers, hearing them and questioning
them; and all who heard him were astonished at his
intelligence and his answers. And seeing him they
were astounded, and his mother said to him,
"Child, why did you do this to us? Behold, your father
and I have been seeking you with great distress!"
And he said to them, "Why did you seek me? Did you
not know that I had to be in the affairs of my Father?"
And they did not understand the word he spoke to them.
And he went down with them and came to Nazareth,
and was subject to them. And his mother carefully
kept all the matters in her heart. And Jesus progressed
in wisdom and age and favor before God and humans.

Antiphon   Son, why have you done this to us?
            But did you not know
            that I had to be in my Father's house?

EVENING PRAYER INTERCESSIONS AND CLOSING PRAYER, see page 271.

CHRISTMAS OCTAVE - December 26
STEPHEN, DEACON & FIRST MARTYR
MORNING

Text: *Saint of God, Elect and Precious,* 11th C.; translated from Latin by John M. Neale, 1852;
adapted by Stephen J. Wolf for the dedication of *St. Stephen Church* on February 2, 2008
Music: 87 87 87 PICARDY, *Chansons Populaires des Provinces de France,* 1860,
Popular melody for *Let All Mortal Flesh Keep Silence*

Ste-phen, dea-con, pro-to\-mar-tyr,
Gift-ed with the Spir-it of God,
Wis-dom, faith and grace, work-ing won-ders,
Speak-ing with an-gel-ic\ word,
Who when dy-ing did   com-mend// to God
Your at-tack-ers with your/ soul.

Tell/, Ste-phen, tell God's\ sto-ry:
Cov-e-nent-ed A-bra\-ham,
Jo-seph res-cued from his af-flic-tion,
Mo-ses raised in Phar-oah's\ land,
At the burn-ing bush,   stand-ing on ho-ly ground,
Sent to set God's peo-ple/ free.

Wear-ing now the crown of a mar-tyr,
In your lang-uage "Crown" your\ name.
You we ask to pray to the Fa-ther
That when we are faced with the same,
We may faith-ful be   free\ from fear and shame
Show-ing mer-cy in God's/ name.

Praise to God and thanks be to Je-sus,
Who has shown us how to for-give,
Pres-ent with the Ho-ly\ Spir-it
They your vis-ion seen as you fell.
Called to serve the poor, then giv-en voice to preach,
Pray we look to heav-en as well.

PSALM 2

Antiphon
Come, let us worship the newborn Christ,
who has given the glorious crown
to Saint Stephen.

Why do nations rage and peoples plot vanity?
Kings of the earth make their stand
and ruling ones gather together
against Adonai and Adonai's anointed one:
"Let us break their chains,
 let us throw off their fetters."

The One enthroned in the heavens laughs,
the Lord scoffs and rebukes them.
In anger and in wrath the Lord terrifies them.
"I indeed installed my king
 on my holy hill of Zion.

PSALM 2, continued

I will proclaim a decree of Adonai who said,
 'You are my son, this day I am your father.
 Ask of me and nations are your inheritance,
 and your possession to the ends of earth.
 You will rule them with a scepter of iron
 and dash them to pieces of what potters make.'

Kings, now be wise!
Rulers of earth, be warned!
Serve Adonai with fear; rejoice with trembling!
Kiss my son, lest he be angry
and you be destroyed
for in a moment he can flare up in wrath.

Blessings on all who take refuge in him."

Glory…

Antiphon — Come, let us worship the newborn Christ,
who has given the glorious crown
to Saint Stephen.

Psalm 63, Daniel 3, and Psalm 149, go to **Christmas Morning**, *page* 16

READING **ACTS 7:54-60**

The brothers and fathers of the Sanhedrin
hearing these things were cut to their hearts
and gnashed their teeth at Stephen.

CHRISTMAS - DEC 26 MORNING

> But being full of the Holy Spirit,
> gazing into heaven he saw the glory of God
> and Jesus standing at the right of God, and said,
> "Behold, I see the heavens opened,
> and the Son of Man standing at the right of God!"
> And crying out with a great voice,
> they closed their ears and rushed on him with one mind,
> and casting outside the city they stoned him.
> The martyr-witnesses put off their garments
> at the feet of a young man called Saul.
> And they stoned Stephen as he called saying,
> "Lord Jesus, receive my spirit."
> And placing his knees he cried with a great voice,
> "Lord, hold not to them this sin!"
> And saying this, he fell asleep.

RESPONSORY

> The Lord is my strength...
> > ...*and I shall sing out praise.*
> The Lord is my Savior...

GOSPEL READING OF THE DAY (or use the **Canticle of Zechariah** from page 268)

Antiphon

Mt 10:17-22

> The gates of heaven
> opened to Stephen,
> crowned the first of the martyrs.

MORNING PRAYER PETITIONS AND CLOSING PRAYER, see page 269.

CHRISTMAS OCTAVE - December 26
EVENING

Si/-**lent night**! Ho/-ly night!
All is calm, all is bright,
Round yon Vir\-gin Moth-er and Child.
Ho-ly In-fant, so ten-der and mild,
Sleep in heav-en-ly peace/,
Sleep\ in heav-en-ly peace.

Si/-lent night! Ho/-ly night!
Shep-herds quake at the sight;
Glo-ries stream\ from heav-en a-far,
Heav'n-ly hosts\ sing, Al-le-lu-ia.
Christ, the Sa-vior is born/!
Christ\, the Sa-vior is born!

Si/-lent night! Ho/-ly night!
Son of God, love's pure light
Ra-diant beams\ form your ho-ly face,
With the dawn of re-deem/-ing grace,
Je-sus, Lord at your birth/,
Je\-sus, Lord at your birth.

Text: Joseph Mohr, 1818; translator unknown, altered
Music: STILLE NACHT, Franz Guber, 1818

PSALM 7

Antiphon Mary and Joseph were filled with wonder
at all that was said of the child.

My God, Adonai, in you I take refuge;
save me and deliver me from all who pursue me.
Like lions they want to tear me up,
rip my self to pieces with no one to rescue me.

My God, Adonai, if I deserve this,
if there is guilt on my hands,
if I did wrong to one at peace with me
or if I robbed without cause from an enemy,
then let that one pursue my self
and overtake my life
and trample my honor to the ground;
let that one put me to sleep in the dust.

Arise, Adonai, rise up in your anger
against the rages of enmity.
Awake, my God, and decree your justice
and let the assembly of peoples surround you;
rule over us from the height.
Let Adonai be the judge of the peoples.

Judge me, Adonai, as you judge me in justice,
as you judge my integrity, Most High.
May violence end now and the righteous be secure;
search our minds and hearts, righteous God.
My shield, God Most High, saves the upright heart,
and judges each day with justice, threatening wrath.

PSALM 7, continued

If none repent, they will sharpen their sword
and bend their bow with string and make ready
with weapons of death and flaming arrows.
See, trouble is conceived and evil is pregnant,
then comes to birth disillusionment.

They dig holes and scoop them out
but fall into the pits they made.
Their trouble recoils on their heads;
on their heads their violence makes landing.

I give thanks for Adonai's righteousness
and sing praise to the name of Most High Adonai.

Glory…

Antiphon   Mary and Joseph were filled with wonder
at all that was said of the child.

Psalm 110, Psalm 130, and Col. 1, go to **Christmas Evening**, *page 29*

READING **1 JOHN 1:5b-7**

God is light,
and in God there is no night,
none.
If we say we have communion with God
and we walk in the darkness,
we lie and are not doing the truth.
But if we walk in the light as God is in the light,
we have communion with each other,
and the blood of Jesus the Son
cleanses us from all sin.

RESPONSORY Jn 1:14

The Word became flesh...
...alleluia, alleluia.
And dwelt among us...

GOSPEL CANTICLE (**Canticle of Mary**) see page 270.

Antiphon While earth was in still quiet silence
and night only half way through,
your almighty Word, O Lord,
came from his royal throne,
alleluia.

EVENING PRAYER INTERCESSIONS AND CLOSING PRAYER, see page 271.

CHRISTMAS OCTAVE - December 27
JOHN, APOSTLE & EVANGELIST
MORNING

Melody: *Morning Has Broken*

As Ab-ba **loves** me   so do I love you.
I tell you this: re-main in my love.
Keep this com-mand-ment: Love one an-oth-er
As I have loved you,   call-ing you friend.

I am the vine and   you are my bran-ches;
Let Ab-ba prune you   so you bear fruit.
My word re-mem-ber: Love one an-oth-er
As I have loved you,   call-ing you friend.

No great-er love than   has one to lay down
One's ver-y life for   e-ven a friend.
You I have cho-sen: Love one an-oth-er
As I have loved you,   call-ing you friend.

You have been with me   from the be-gin-ning;
Tes-ti-fy in the   Spir-it of truth.
In word and ac-tion: Love one an-oth-er
As I have loved you,   call-ing you friend.

Text: from John 15, Stephen J. Wolf, 2007, tribute to the priesthood of Charley Giacosa
Music: BUNESSAN 5554 D, Scots Gaelic melody
Popular melody for: *Morning Has Broken*

PSALM 99

Antiphon Come, let us worship the Lord,
the King of apostles.

Adonai reigns; let the nations tremble.
The One sits enthroned on the cherubim;
let the earth shake.

Great in Zion is Adonai,
and exalted over all of the nations.
Let them praise your great and awesome name,
"Holy are you, and mighty."

The King of justice loves you
and establishes equity and justice,
having done what is right in Jacob.

Exalt Adonai our God!
And worship at the feet on the footstool,
"Holy are you, and mighty."

Moses and Aaron are among the priests,
and Samuel among those calling the name,
calling on El Adonai, who answered them,
who spoke to them from the pillar of cloud.
They kept the statutes and decrees given to them.

Adonai, our God, you answered them.
You were the one Forgiving El to them,
though punishing their misdeeds.

PSALM 99, continued

> Exalt Adonai our God!
> And worship at the holy mountain,
> for holy is our God Adonai!

Glory...

Antiphon Come, let us worship the Lord,
the King of apostles.

Psalm 63, Daniel 3, and Psalm 149, go to **Christmas Morning** *, page* 16

READING **ACTS 4:19-20**

> Peter and John answering said to them,
> "If it is right before God
> to hear you rather than God,
> you decide.
> For ourselves, we cannot but speak
> of the things which we saw and heard"

RESPONSORY

> You have made them rulers...
> *...over all the earth.*
> They will always remember your name, O Lord...

GOSPEL READING OF THE DAY (or use the **Canticle of Zechariah** from page 268)

Antiphon The Word became flesh
Jn 20:1a,2-8 and pitched his tent among us
and we have seen his glory.

MORNING PRAYER PETITIONS AND CLOSING PRAYER, see page 269.

CHRISTMAS OCTAVE - December 27
EVENING

Melody: *All Creatures of Our God and King*

God, our/ ref-uge and our strength,
Ev-er/ pres-ent help in stress.
God is with us, thus we fear not.
Though the\ earth and moun-tains shake,
Deep of\ wa-ters foam and rage,
Moun-tains tot-ter, wa-ter surg-ing,
God of Ja-cob is our strong-hold, God is with.. us.

Ho-ly/ dwell-ing of our God,
Stream-ing/ riv-er glad-den there
In the cit-y of our ref-uge.
Na-tions\ rage and king-doms fall,
All earth\ trem-bles at the call,
God will help at break of new day,
God of Ja-cob is our strong-hold, God is with.. us.

"**B**e still and know that I am God."
Come and/ see the works of God:
Stop-ping war in ev-'ry na-tion,
Break-ing\ weap-on, break-ing spear,
Burn-ing\ bow and ar-mor shield,
Say-ing, "Be still, know your God now,"
God of Ja-cob is our strong-hold, God is with.. us.

Text: from Psalm 46, by Stephen J. Wolf, 2003, tribute to the priesthood of Joseph Wesley
Music: LASST UNS ERFREUEN, LM with alleluias; *Geistliche Kirchengesange,* 1623

PSALM 7

Antiphon Mary and Joseph were filled with wonder
at all that was said of the child.

My God, Adonai, in you I take refuge;
save me and deliver me from all who pursue me.
Like lions they want to tear me up,
rip my self to pieces with no one to rescue me.

My God, Adonai, if I deserve this,
if there is guilt on my hands,
if I did wrong to one at peace with me
or if I robbed without cause from an enemy,
then let that one pursue my self
and overtake my life
and trample my honor to the ground;
let that one put me to sleep in the dust.

Arise, Adonai, rise up in your anger
against the rages of enmity.
Awake, my God, and decree your justice
and let the assembly of peoples surround you;
rule over us from the height.
Let Adonai be the judge of the peoples.

Judge me, Adonai, as you judge me in justice,
as you judge my integrity, Most High.
May violence end now and the righteous be secure;
search our minds and hearts, righteous God.
My shield, God Most High, saves the upright heart,
and judges each day with justice, threatening wrath.

If none repent, they will sharpen their sword
and bend their bow with string and make ready
with weapons of death and flaming arrows.
See, trouble is conceived and evil is pregnant,
then comes to birth disillusionment.

They dig holes and scoop them out
but fall into the pits they made.
Their trouble recoils on their heads;
on their heads their violence makes landing.

I give thanks for Adonai's righteousness
and sing praise to the name of Most High Adonai.

Glory...

Antiphon Mary and Joseph were filled with wonder
at all that was said of the child.

Psalm 110, Psalm 130, and Col. 1, go to **Christmas Evening**, *page 29*

READING — **ROMANS 8:3-4**

God sent God's own Son in the likeness of sinful flesh
condemning sin in the flesh,
that the ordering of the law might be fulfilled in us,
walking not in accord with the flesh
but in accord with the Spirit.

RESPONSORY — Jn 1:14

The Word became flesh…
…*alleluia, alleluia.*
And dwelt among us…

GOSPEL CANTICLE (**Canticle of Mary**) see page 270.

Antiphon

Virgin Mary,
all the prophets foretold of the Christ
is now fulfilled through you:
as a virgin, you conceived
and after you gave birth
a virgin you remained.

EVENING PRAYER INTERCESSIONS AND CLOSING PRAYER, see page 271.

CHRISTMAS OCTAVE - December 28
THE HOLY INNOCENTS
MORNING

A migh-ty for/-tress is\ our God,
    The bul-wark nev-er fail\\-ing;
Our help-er, God/, a-mid\ the flood
    Of mor-tal ills pre-vail\\-ing:
For still/ our an-cient\ foe
    Does seek to work us woe;
His craft and pow'r are great,
    And armed with cru-el hate,
    On earth is not his e\\-qual.

Do we in our/ own strength\ con-fide?
    Our stri-ving would be los\\-ing,
Were not the Sa/-vior on\ our side,
    The Son of God's own choos\\-ing:
You ask/ who that may\ be?
    Christ Je-sus, it is he;
Lord Sab-a-oth, his name,
    From age to age the same,
    And he must win the bat\\-tle.

Text: based on Psalm 46; Martin Luther, 1529;
translated by Frederick H. Hedge, d.1890, altered
Music: 87 87 66 66 7 EIN' FESTE BURG; Martin Luther, 1529

PSALM 33

Antiphon	Come, let us worship the newborn Christ
who crowns with joy
these children who died for him.

Sing joyfully to Adonai, righteous ones,
for praise is fitting for the upright.

Praise Adonai with a harp,
make music on the lyre of ten.
Sing a new song with skill
and play with a shout of joy.

For right is the word of Adonai
and all the faithful deeds done.
Loving righteousness and justice,
the earth is full of Adonai's unfailing love.

The heavens were made by the word of Adonai
and all their hosts by the breath of this mouth,
as one gathers in a heap the waters of the sea,
as one puts into the deep of the storehouses.

Let all the earth, let them fear,
let all alive in the world revere Adonai
who spoke and it came to be,
who commanded and it stood firm.

Adonai foils the plans of the nations
and thwarts the purposes of peoples.
The plan of Adonai stands firm to forever,
heartfelt purpose to generation and generation.

Blessed is the nation for whom Adonai is God,
the people chosen for this inheritance.
From the heavens Adonai looks down and sees
all sons and daughters of Adam and Eve,

and from the place of dwelling watches
all those alive on the earth.
The one who formed our heart
considers all our deeds.

No king is saved by the size of an army;
no warrior escapes by greatness of strength.
The horse is a vain hope for deliverance;
despite greatness of strength it cannot save.

See the eye of Adonai on those who place
their fear and hope in the unfailing love
that delivers them from death
and keeps them alive in the famine.

Our being waits for Adonai,
who is our help and our shield,
in whom our heart rejoices,
the holy name in whom we trust.

Adonai, may you rest on us your unfailing love
even as we hope in you.

Glory…

Antiphon   Come, let us worship the newborn Christ
who crowns with joy
these children who died for him.

Psalm 63, Daniel 3, and Psalm 149, go to **Christmas Morning**, *page* 16

READING   **MATTHEW 2:13-18**

When they had departed,
behold an angel of the Lord appeared by a dream
to Joseph saying,
"Rise, take the child and his mother,
and flee into Egypt, and be there until I tell you,
for Herod is about to seek the child to destroy him."
So rising he took the child and his mother
and departed by night to Egypt,
and was there until the death of Herod,
that might be fulfilled what was spoken by the Lord
through the prophet saying,
Out of Egypt I called my son.
Then Herod, seeing that he was mocked by the magi,
was exceedingly angry,
and sending killed all the boy-children
from two years and under in Bethlehem
and in all its districts, according to the time
which he strictly inquired from the magi.
Then was fulfilled what was spoken
through Jeremiah the prophet saying,

CHRISTMAS - DEC 28 MORNING

A voice in Ramah was heard,
weeping and much mourning,
Rachel weeping for her children,
and would not be comforted
because they are not.

RESPONSORY

The just are the friends of God...
...They live with him for ever.
God's own self is their reward...

GOSPEL CANTICLE (**Canticle of Zechariah**) see page 268.

Antiphon

At the command of a king
innocent babies and children
died in the place of Christ;
now in the glory of heaven
they follow the sinless Lamb
and sing forever:
Glory to you, O Lord.

MORNING PRAYER PETITIONS AND CLOSING PRAYER, see page 269.

CHRISTMAS OCTAVE - December 28
EVENING

To you we owe our hymn of praise,
Bur-dened with sin your peo-ples come.
You hear our prayer, O God of Zi\-on;
Vows kept and bro-ken, made a-new.

Still ov-er-come are we by sin,
Lord you a-lone can par-don them.
Hap-py the cho-sen ones you bring with-in
Your tem-ple court with good things giv'n.

You an-swer us with awe-some deed,
Jus-tice and hope to ends of earth.
You still the roar-ing of the wave and sea;
Set up the moun-tains by your might.

You still the tu-mult of the crowd,
Now east and west re-sound with joy.
Peo-ple in lands and is-lands far a-way,
See-ing your mar-vel stand in awe.

You vis-it earth and wa-ter her,
Ma-king a-bun-dant streams of life.
God's fer-tile earth pre-pared is blessed in rain,
God's world sup-plied for fields of grain.

Lord, you are hope for all the earth,
You hear the hum-ble sing your praise.
Choose us a-gain, pour out your Spir-it free;
Bear fruit in us that all may see.

Text: from Psalm 65 of the New American Bible, by Stephen J. Wolf, 2003,
tribute to the priesthood of George Rohling
Music: JESU DULCIS MEMORIA, LM; Model 1;
Popular melody for: *O Radiant Light, O Sun Divine*

HINGE HOURS for CHRISTMAS

PSALM 17

Antiphon
        My own eyes have seen
        the salvation which you have prepared
        in the sight of every people.

Hear, Adonai, a righteous plea; listen to my cry.
Give ear to my prayer, from lips without deceit.
May my vindication come from you;
may my eyes see right things.

You probe and examine my heart in the night,
you test me and will find nothing.
By resolve my mouth will not sin.

By the word of your lips
my human deeds are kept from violent ways.
Holding my steps to your paths my feet did not slip.

I call on you, El, for you will answer me.
Give your ear to me and hear my prayer.
Show the wonder of your great saving love,
at your right hand those taking refuge from foes.

Keep me as the apple daughter of your eye.
You hide me in the shade of your wings
from those who assail me in enmity,
surrounding around my life.
They close their callous hearts,
they speak their arrogant mouth.

PSALM 17, continued

Now they surround our tracks;
their eyes are alert, ready to throw to the ground.
They are like a lion, hungry to tear prey,
like a great lion crouching undercover.

Rise up, Adonai!
Confront and bring down their ways.
Rescue my self by your sword, Adonai,
by your hand from humans,
humans of the world whose reward is this life.

As for those who are cherished by you,
their belly is full, sons and daughters are plenty,
and they store up their wealth for their children.

In justice, I will see your faces
and be satisfied waking up to your likeness.

Glory…

Antiphon

My own eyes have seen
the salvation which you have prepared
in the sight of every people.

Psalm 110, Psalm 130, and Col. 1, go to **Christmas Evening***, page 29*

CHRISTMAS - DEC 28 EVENING

READING   **EPHESIANS 2:3b-5**

As the rest,
we also were by nature children of anger.
But being rich in mercy
because of the great agape-love
with which God loved us,
even when we were dead in trespasses
God raised us with Christ.
By grace you have been saved.

RESPONSORY   Jn 1:14

The Word became flesh...
                ...*alleluia, alleluia.*
And dwelt among us...

GOSPEL CANTICLE (**Canticle of Mary**) see page 270.

Antiphon   The holy Virgin gave birth to God
who became for us
the vulnerable baby
nursed at her breast.
Let us worship the Lord
who comes to save us.

EVENING PRAYER INTERCESSIONS AND CLOSING PRAYER, see page 271.

CHRISTMAS OCTAVE - December 29
MORNING

How love-ly is_   your dwell-ing place,
O Lord of hosts_!   Be-lov-ed\ Lord!
My soul does yearn_   for the liv-ing God.
Bod-y and soul_   cry out, "my God!"

The spar-row finds_   a home to rest,
The swal-low too_   a set-tled\ nest,
The mock-ing-bird_   her\ place to sing:
"My home is with_   my God and King!"

Pass-ing through val_   -leys, hills and springs
And pools of wa_   -ter for the\ lost;
Hap-py in ref_   -uge\ pil-grims bring
Good news of God_,   our Lord and King.

Hap-py then are_   your pil-grims all,
Hearts long-ing to_   see tem-ple\ walls.
Bet-ter is one_   day\ in your courts
Than thou-sands far_   from Ja-cob's Lord.

O Lord of hosts_,   come hear our prayer.
Look on the face_   your'a-noint-ed\ bear:
Hap-py are we_   who\ trust and hope
In you, Be-lov_   -ed Lord of Hosts!

Text: from Psalm 84, by Stephen J. Wolf, 2007, tribute to Thomas Merton
Music: O WALY WALY, LM; traditional English tune;
Popular melody for: *As The Deer Longs For Flowing Streams*

PSALM 46

Antiphon Christ is born for us;
come let us adore him.

God is our refuge and strength,
our help in troubles, ever present.
And so we will not fear,
even if earth were to give way,
even if mountains were to fall
into the heart of the sea,
even if sea waters foam
or mountains quake with that surging.

A river has streams that make glad God's city,
the holy dwelling place of the Most High.
God is inside her and she will not fall.
God will help her at the break of day.
Nations are in uproar, kingdoms fall;
the earth melts at the voice of God.

Adonai Sabaoth is with us;
the God of Jacob is our fortress.

Come and see the works of Adonai,
the desolations brought on the earth:
making wars to cease to the ends of the earth,
breaking the bow and shattering the spear
and burning with fire the chariot and shield.

"Be still! And know that I am God.
 I will be exalted among the nations;
 I will be exalted on the earth."

PSALM 46, continued

Adonai Sabaoth is with us;
the God of Jacob is our fortress.

Glory…

Antiphon Christ is born for us;
come let us adore him.

Psalm 63, Daniel 3, and Psalm 149, go to **Christmas Morning**, *page* 16

READING **HEBREWS 1:1-2**

Of old, having spoken to the ancestors by the prophets
often and in many ways,
in these last days God spoke to us in a Son,
appointed as heir of all things,
and indeed through whom God made the eons.

RESPONSORY

The Lord has made known…
…*alleluia, alleluia.*
His saving power.

GOSPEL READING OF THE DAY (or use the **Canticle of Zechariah** from page 268)

Antiphon The shepherds said to one another:
Luke 2:22-35 Let us go then to Bethlehem
and see this thing happening
which the Lord has made known to us.

MORNING PRAYER PETITIONS AND CLOSING PRAYER, see page 269.

CHRISTMAS OCTAVE - December 29
EVENING

It came up-on\ the mid-night clear,
That glo/-rious song/ of old,
From an-gels bend\-ing near the earth,
To touch their harps\ of gold;
"Peace on the earth/, good will to all,
From heav-en's all gra/-cious King."
The world in sol\-emn still-ness lay,
To hear the an\-gels sing.

To you, be-neath\ life's crush-ing load,
Whose forms/ are bend/-ing low,
Who toil a-long\ the climb-ing way
With pain-ful steps\ and slow,
Look now! for glad/ and gol-den hours
Come swift\-ly on/ the wing.
O rest be-side\ the wea-ry road,
And hear the an\-gels sing.

For lo! the days\ are hast'n-ing on,
By pro/-phet-bards/ fore-told,
When with the ev\-er circ-ling years
Come round the age of gold;
When peace shall o/-ver all the earth
Its an\-cient splen/-dors fling,
And the whole world\ send back the song
Which now the an\-gels sing.

Text: Edmund H. Sears, 1849   Music: CAROL CMD, Richard S. Willis, 1850

PSALM 25

Antiphon   Mary and Joseph were filled with wonder
at all that was said of the child.

To you, Adonai, I lift up my soul;
in you, my God, I trust;
let me not be shamed
and let enmity not triumph over me.
Indeed all who hope in you will not be shamed;
shamed will be those doing defenseless treachery.

Show me your ways, Adonai; teach me your paths.
Guide me in your truth and teach me,
for you are my saving God;
you are my hope all the day.

Remember your mercies, Adonai,
and your loves, for they are from of old.
The sins of my youth and rebellious ways
you do not remember, as you are loving.

You do remember me, for you are good, Adonai.
Good and upright is Adonai,
who instructs sinners in the way,
guides humble ones in rightness,
and teaches the way to the humble.

All the ways of Adonai are loving and faithful
for those who keep the covenant demands.
For the sake of your name, Adonai,
now you forgive my iniquity, great as it is.

Who is the human who fears Adonai?
The one being instructed in the Lord's chosen way,
whose life will be days spent in prosperity,
whose descendants will inherit the land,
the confidence of Adonai is with those thus fearing;
the covenant is made known to them.

My eyes are ever on Adonai,
who will release my feet from the snare.
Turn to me! Be gracious to me!
For I am lonely and afflicted.

Troubles of my heart have multiplied;
free me from my anguish!
Look upon my affliction and distress!
Take away all of my sins!

See the enmity,
the increase of fierce hate!
Guard my life! Rescue me!
Let me not be shamed, for I take refuge in you.
May integrity and uprightness protect me
because I hope in you.

Redeem Israel, God, from all our troubles.

Glory...

Antiphon — Mary and Joseph were filled with wonder
at all that was said of the child.

*Psalm 110, Psalm 130, and Col. 1, go to **Christmas Evening**, page 29*

READING   **1 JOHN 1:1-3**

What was from the beginning,
what we have heard,
what we have seen with our eyes,
what we have looked at and our hands have touched
concerning the Word of Life,
and the life has been shown,
we have seen and we bear witness
and we proclaim to you the life eternal,
which was with the Father and has been shown to us.
What we have seen and heard, we proclaim also to you
that you also may have communion with us.
Indeed our communion is with the Father
and with the Son, Jesus Christ.

RESPONSORY   Jn 1:14

The Word became flesh…
…*alleluia, alleluia.*
And dwelt among us…

GOSPEL CANTICLE (**Canticle of Mary**) see page 270.

Antiphon   The King of heaven took on humility,
                    born of a virgin
                    to restore to all humanity
                    the kingdom humanity lost.

EVENING PRAYER INTERCESSIONS AND CLOSING PRAYER, see page 271.

CHRISTMAS OCTAVE - December 30
MORNING

God rest ye mer-ry, gen-tle-men,
   let noth-ing you dis-may,
Re-mem-ber Christ our Sa\-vior
   was born on Christ-mas day;
To save us from the e-vil pow'r
   when we had gone a-stray.

Refrain   O/ ti-dings of com\-fort and joy,
        com-fort and joy;
        O/ ti/-dings of com\-fort and joy.

From God our heav'n-ly Fa\-ther
   a bless-ed an-gel came;
And un-to cer-tain shep\-herds
   brought ti-dings of the same;
How that in Beth-le-hem was born
   the Son of God by name...   *Refrain*

"So, have no fear," the an-gel said,
   "but find the vir-gin maid.
Of her is born the Sa\-vior,
   so do not be afraid.
Now free are all who trus-ted their
   re-demp-tion would be paid"...   *Refrain*

Text: traditional English Carol, 18th C., altered
Music: 86 86 86 with refrain GOD REST YOU MERRY,
from *Little Book of Christmas Carols*, 1846

PSALM 85

Antiphon Christ is born for us;
come let us adore him.

You showed favor, Adonai, to your land;
you restored the fortune of Jacob.
You forgave the iniquity of your people;
you covered all of their sin.
You set aside all of your wrath;
you turned from your fierce anger.

Restore us, God of our salvation!
And put away your displeasure toward us.
Will you be angry with us to forever?
Will you prolong your anger
to generation and generation?

Will you not revive us again
that your people may rejoice in you?
Show us, Adonai, your unfailing love
and grant us your salvation.

I will listen to what El Adonai will say,
promising peace to the people, even to the saints,
but not letting them return to folly.
Surely near to ones fearing is salvation,
the glory to dwell in our land.

Love and Faithfulness meet;
Justice and Peace kiss.
Faithfulness springs forth from the earth
and Justice looks down from the heavens.

CHRISTMAS - DEC 30 MORNING

Indeed Adonai will give the good
and our land will yield her harvest,
Justice going forward to prepare
the way for the steps of the Lord.

Glory...

Antiphon   Christ is born for us;
            come let us adore him.

Psalm 63, Daniel 3, and Psalm 149, go to **Christmas Morning** *, page* 16

READING   **ISAIAH 9:4-6**

Every boot of a warrior in battle
and garment rolled in blood
will then be for burning, for fuel in fire,
for a child is born to us, a son is given to us,
and the governing will be on his shoulders.
And his name will be called Wonder-Counselor,
God of Might, Father-Everlasting, Prince of Peace.
No end to the increase of governing and of peace,
the throne of David is established over the kingdom
to be upheld with justice and with righteousness
from now and to forever.
The zeal of Adonai Sabaoth will accomplish this.

RESPONSORY

The Lord has made known...

...alleluia, alleluia.

His saving power.

GOSPEL READING OF THE DAY (or use the **Canticle of Zechariah** from page 268)

Antiphon	At the birth of the Lord
Luke 2:36-40	the choirs of angels sang:
	Blessed be our God enthroned as King
	and blessed be the Lamb.

MORNING PRAYER PETITIONS AND CLOSING PRAYER, see page 269.

CHRISTMAS OCTAVE - December 30
EVENING

Melody: *Let All Mortal Flesh Keep Silence*

Face to face with all who would be "gods,"
Our God ri-ses and judge-ment gives:
"How long will you judge with-out jus-tice?"
Asks the One true God who\ lives,
"How long will you give
To those with pow'r and means
All your fa-vor, judge-ment, and will?"

"**Y**ou who would be "gods," seek-ing pow-er,
Nei-ther know nor un-der\-stand,
Wan-der-ing the land, walk in dark-ness,
Shake the world's foun-da-tion a-round;
'gods' though you would be,
Off-spring of the Most High,
Your lives, mor-tal prin-ces, will end."

If you would be God's judg-ing ser-vant,
Ren-der jus-tice to God's own poor,
Keep-ing safe from all who would harm them,
Or-phans, wid-ows, strang-ers and more.
To the low-ly and   peo-ple af-flict\-ed
Give their due of earth's fruit and store.

Text: from Psalm 82 of the New American Bible, by Stephen J. Wolf, 2007,
tribute to the priesthood of Bishop James Neidergeses
Music: 87 87 87 PICARDY, *Chansons Populaires des Provinces de France,* 1860

PSALM 89:*2-38*

Antiphon

Mary treasured all these words
and pondered them in her heart.

Forever will I sing the great love of Adonai;
with my mouth I will make known
your faithfulness to generation and generation.
Indeed I will declare forever love standing firm,
your faithfulness established in the heavens.

"I made a covenant with my chosen ones,
 sworn to my servant David.
 I will establish your line to forever,
 and to generation and generation
 I will make firm your throne."

The heavens praise your wonder, Adonai,
and your faithfulness in the holy assembly.
For who in the sky can compare to Adonai;
who is like Adonai among heavenly beings?

God is greatly feared in the council of holy ones
and is awesome over all who surround around.
Adonai Sabaoth, who is like you?
Mighty Adonai, your faithfulness is around you.

You rule over the surging of the sea;
when waves mount up you still them.
You crushed Rahab like the slain
and scattered enmity
with the arm of your strength.

To you are the heavens and to you is the earth;
the world and her fullness you founded.
North and South you created;
Tabor and Hermon sing for joy at your name.

To you is the arm strong with power;
your hand is exalted, your right hand.
Righteousness and Justice
are the foundation of your throne;
Hesed-Love and Faithfulness go before your faces.

Blessed are people who learn to acclaim Adonai;
they walk in the light of your presences.
In your name they rejoice all the day
and in your righteousness they exult,

for you are the glory of their strength
and by your favor you exalt our horn.
Indeed Adonai is our shield
and the Holy One of Israel is our king.

Once in a vision you spoke to your faithful ones:
"I bestowed strength on a warrior;
 I exalted from the people a young man.

 I found David my servant,
 I anointed him with my sacred oil,
 and my hand will sustain him;
 surely my arm will strengthen him.

 No enemy will subject him to tribute
 and no wicked people will oppress him.
 Before him I will crush foes
 and strike down adversity,

PSALM 89:2-38, continued

and my faithfulness and my love are with him,
and through my hands will the horn be exalted.
And I will set his hand over the sea
and his right hand over the rivers.

He will call me out: 'You are my Father,
  my God and Rock of my salvation.'
I will also appoint him firstborn
and most exalted among kings of the earth.

I will maintain my love for him to forever
and my unfailing covenant with him.
I will establish his line to forever
and his throne as days of the heavens.

If his sons and daughters forsake my law
and do not follow my statutes,
if they violate my decrees
and keep not my commands,

then I will punish their sins with the rod
and their iniquity with floggings.
But I will not take my love from them,
nor will I ever betray my faithfulness.

I will not violate my covenant
nor will I alter the utterance of my lips.
Once I swore by my holiness;
I will not lie to David:

His line will continue to forever
and his throne like the sun before me.
Like the moon it is established forever,
a faithful witness in the sky."

CHRISTMAS - DEC 30 EVENING

Glory...

Antiphon   Mary treasured all these words
and pondered them in her heart.

Psalm 110, Psalm 130, and Col. 1, go to **Christmas Evening**, *page 29*

READING   **2 PETER 1:3-4**

The divine power has given us
all things that go with life and piety
through the full knowledge
of the one who called us to this glory and virtue,
through which the precious things
and the very great promises
have been given to us,
so that through these you might escape
from the corruption of worldly desire
and come to share in the divine nature.

RESPONSORY   Jn 1:14

The Word became flesh...
                ...*alleluia, alleluia.*
And dwelt among us...

GOSPEL CANTICLE (**Canticle of Mary**) see page 270.

Antiphon   We join the communion of saints
in a grateful song to the Mother of God
who gave birth to our Savior, Jesus Christ;
watch over all who honor you.

EVENING PRAYER INTERCESSIONS AND CLOSING PRAYER, see page 271.

CHRISTMAS OCTAVE - December **31**
MORNING

There's a star in the East on/ Christ-mas morn,
Rise up, shep-herd, and fol-low.
It will lead to the place
      where the Christ was born\\,
Rise up, shep-herd, and fol-low.

Refrain   **Fol**/-low, fol\-low,
              Rise up, shep-herd, and fol-low.
              Fol-low the Star of Beth-le-hem\\,
              Rise up, shep-herd, and fol-low.

If you take good\ heed to the an-gel's words,
Rise up, shep-herd, and fol-low.
You'll for-get your\ flocks,
      you'll for-get your herds\\\,
Rise up, shep-herd, and fol-low.

Refrain

Text: African-American spiritual
Music: 10 7 11 7 with refrain

PSALM 96

Antiphon Christ is born for us;
come let us adore him.

Sing to Adonai a new song!
Sing to Adonai, all the earth!
Sing to Adonai and praise the name!
Proclaim the salvation from day to day!

Declare among the nations the glory of the Lord!
Among all the peoples the marvelous deeds,
for great is Adonai, greatly being praised,
the one being feared above all so-called "gods."

For all "gods" of the nations are idols,
but Adonai made the heavens,
splendor and majesty and strength and glory
in the holy sanctuary.

Ascribe to Adonai, families of nations!
Ascribe to Adonai glory and strength!
Ascribe to Adonai the glory of the name!

Bring offerings and come into the courts!
Worship Adonai in holy splendor!
Tremble in the presence all the earth!

Say among the nations, "Adonai reigns!"
Firmly established, the world cannot be moved
and peoples will be judged with equity.

PSALM 96, continued

Let the heavens rejoice and the earth be glad.
Let the sea resound and all its fullness.
Let the fields and all that is in them be jubilant,
then all the trees of the forests will sing for joy

before Adonai who comes,
who comes to judge the earth,
who will judge the world and its peoples
in justice and in truth.

Glory…

Antiphon   Christ is born for us;
                  come let us adore him.

Psalm 63, Daniel 3, and Psalm 149, go to **Christmas Morning** *, page* 16

CHRISTMAS - DEC 31 MORNING

READING **ISAIAH 4:2-3**

In that day the Branch of Adonai
will be beauty and glory
and the fruit of the land
the pride and glory of survivors in Israel.
And the ones being left and remaining in Jerusalem
will be called holy,
all recorded among the living in Jerusalem.

RESPONSORY

The Lord has made known...
...alleluia, alleluia.
His saving power.

GOSPEL READING OF THE DAY (or use the **Canticle of Zechariah** from page 268)

AntiphonSuddenly there was with the angel
John 1:1-18a multitude of the heavenly hosts,
praising God and singing:
Glory to God in the highest
and peace on earth to the people of God,
alleluia.

MORNING PRAYER PETITIONS AND CLOSING PRAYER, see page 269.

CHRISTMAS OCTAVE - Vigil of Jan. 1
THEOTOKOS, MARY the MOTHER of GOD
EVENING

Vir-gin-born, we bow be-fore you;
Bless-ed was the womb that bore you:
Ma-ry, Moth-er meek and mild.

Bless-ed was the maid that fed you;
Bless-ed was the hand that led you;
Watch-ing you, the in-fant child.

Bless-ed she by all cre-a-tion,
Who brought forth the world's sal-va-tion;
Bless-ed was her par-ent style.

Bless-ed was she in her Chi-ld.
Bless-ed they for-ev-er blest, who
Love you most and serve you while.

Vir-gin-born, we bow be-fore you;
Bless-ed was the womb that bore you:
Mary, Moth-er meek and mild.

Text: Reginald Heber, d.1826, altered for a different tune
Music: 88 7 STABAT MATER, *Mainz Gesanbuch,* 1661

PSALM 34

Antiphon My own eyes have seen the salvation
prepared by you for every people to see.

I will extol Adonai at all times,
praise always on my lips.
My soul she will boast in Adonai,
let afflicted ones hear and let them rejoice.

Glorify Adonai with me!
Let us exalt the name together.
I sought Adonai, who answered me
and delivered me from all my fears.

They look to the name and are radiant;
their faces are never covered with shame.
This poor human called and Adonai heard,
and saved this one from all troubles.

An angel encamps around those who fear Adonai
and delivers them.
Taste and see that Adonai is good!
Blessed is the one who takes this refuge.

Fear Adonai, you saints;
for those who do so there is no lack.
Lions may grow weak and may grow hungry,
but seekers of Adonai lack no good thing.

PSALM 34, continued

Come, children! Listen to me!
I will teach you the fear of Adonai.
Who is the human who loves living?
Who desires days to see the good?

Keep your tongue from evil
and your lips from speaking the lie.
Turn from evil! And do good!
Seek and pursue peace!

The eyes of Adonai are on righteous ones
with ears open to their cry.
The faces of Adonai turn from those doing evil
to cut off from the earth their memory.

They cry and Adonai hears
and delivers them from all their troubles.
Close is Adonai to the brokenhearted,
saving those whose spirit is crushed.

Many are the troubles of the righteous
but Adonai delivers them from all of them,
protecting all of their bones;
not one of them will be broken.

Evil will slay the wicked and condemned will be
those who stay foes of the righteous.
The servants of Adonai are being redeemed
and the lives of any who take this refuge
will not be condemned.

Glory...

Antiphon   My own eyes have seen the salvation
prepared by you for every people to see.

PSALM 113

Antiphon

O marvelous exchange! Humanity's Creator
has become human, born of a virgin.
We have been made sharers in the divinity
of Christ who humbled himself
to share in our humanity.

Hallelujah! Praise Adonai!
Praise, you who serve Adonai!
Praise the name Adonai!

Let Adonai be praised by name
from now and to forevermore.
From the rising of the sun to its setting
praised be the name Adonai.

Exalted over all the nations is Adonai,
the glory above the heavens.
Who is like our God Adonai,
sitting enthroned on high,
leaning to look down
on the heavens and the earth?

The One who raises the poor from dust
and lifts up the needy from ash heaps
to sit with princes, the princes of the people,
who settles the barren woman in a home,
a happy mother of children.

Hallelujah! Praise Adonai!

Glory…

Repeat antiphon.

PSALM 147:12-20

Antiphon

By your miraculous birth of the Virgin
you have fulfilled the Scriptures:
like a gentle rain falling upon the earth
you have come to save your people.
O God, we praise you.

Extol Adonai, Jerusalem!
Zion, now give praise!

Your God strengthens the bars of your gates,
blesses your peoples within you,
grants peace to your border,
and satisfies you with finest of wheat.

Your God sends a command to the earth,
and in swiftness runs a word,
spreading snow like the wool
and scattering frost like the ash.

Hail is hurled like pebbles;
who can stand before the icy blast?
The word of the Lord is sent, and they melt;
wind stirs up and the waters flow.

The word of the Lord is revealed to Jacob,
decrees and laws of the Lord to Israel.
Not for any nation did the Lord do this;
they do not know these laws.
Hallelujah! Praise Adonai!

Glory...

Repeat antiphon.

EPHESIANS 1:3-10

Antiphon
>Your blessed and fruitful virginity
>is like the bush Moses saw on Sinai, flaming
>yet unburned. Pray for us, Mother of God.

Blessed be the God and Father
of our Lord Jesus Christ,
who has blessed us in Christ
with every spiritual blessing in the heavens.

God chose us in Christ
before the foundation of the world,
to be holy and free of blemish before him.

In love, God gave us a destiny:
as sons are adopted, through Jesus Christ himself,
in accord with the good pleasure of God's will
to the praise of the glory of grace
by which we are favored as God's beloved.

In Christ we have the redemption
through his blood, the forgiveness of sins,
in accord with the riches of his grace
which he made abound to us.

In all wisdom and intelligence
the mystery of God's will is made known to us
in accord with God's good pleasure and purpose:

A stewardship of the fullness of time,
heading up all things in Christ,
the things in the heavens and the things on earth.

Glory... Repeat antiphon.

READING **GALATIANS 4:4-5**

God sent forth God's own Son,
becoming of a woman, becoming under the law,
that he might redeem those under the law,
that we might receive the full adoption
as sons and daughters.
And because we are sons and daughters,
God sent forth the Spirit of the Son of God
into our hearts, crying, "Abba, Father."

RESPONSORY   Jn 1:14

The Word became flesh...
...alleluia, alleluia.
And dwelt among us...

GOSPEL CANTICLE (**Canticle of Mary**) see page 270.

Antiphon   In God's great love for us,
the Son of God is sent
in the likeness of our nature,
born too of a woman
and with us subject to the law,
alleluia.

EVENING PRAYER INTERCESSIONS AND CLOSING PRAYER, see page 271.

CHRISTMAS OCTAVE - JANUARY 1
THEOTOKOS, MARY the MOTHER of GOD
MORNING

Melody: *Sing of Mary, Pure and Lowly*

Hark, a\ thrill-ing/ voice is sound-ing!
"Christ is\ nigh!" we/ hear it say;
"Cast a\-way the/ works of dark-ness,
O ye\ chil-dren/ of the day."
Star-tled\ at the sol-emn\ warn-ing,
Let the\ earth-bound soul a\-rise;
Christ, her\ Sun, all/ sloth dis-pel-ling,
Shines up\-on the/ morn-ing skies.

Lo, the\ Lamb, so/ long ex-pect-ed,
Comes with\ par-don/ from a-bove.
Let us\ haste to ap-proach his mer-cy
Draw-ing\ near with/ words of love.
Hon-or\, glo-ry, might, do\-min-ion,
To the\ Fa-ther and the\ Son,
With the\ e-ver/-last-ing Spir-it,
While e\-ter-nal/ ages run!

Text: see Rom 13:11; unknown author, c. 900;
translated by Edward Caswall, 1849, altered
Music: 87 87 D, PLEADING SAVIOR, Joshua Leavitt, *Christian Lyre,* 1830
Popular melody for: *Sing of Mary, Pure and Lowly*

PSALM 87

Antiphon   Let us celebrate the motherhood of Mary;
let us worship her Son, Christ the Lord.

On the holy mountain is the foundation of Adonai,
who loves the gates of Zion
more than all of Jacob's dwellings.
Glorious things are being said of you, city of God.

"I will record Rahab and Babylon
 among those who know me;
 see Philistia and Tyre with Cush:
 this one was born there!"

Indeed of Zion it will be said,
"One and another were born in her,
 and the Most High will establish her."
Adonai will write when registering peoples,
"This one was born there."
And making music the ones will sing,
"All of my fountains are in you."

Glory…

Antiphon   Let us celebrate the motherhood of Mary;
let us worship her Son, Christ the Lord.

Psalm 63, Daniel 3, and Psalm 149, go to **Christmas Morning** *, page* 16

CHRISTMAS - JAN 1 MORNING

READING **MICAH 5:1-4a,6**

But you, Beth Lehem Ephrathah,
small among clans of Judah,
from you will come out one to rule over Israel,
his goings out from of old, from days of ancient times.
And so they will abandon Israel until
the time of her being in labor and she gives birth,
and the rest of the brothers will return
to the peoples of Israel.
He will stand and shepherd in the strength of Adonai,
in the majesty of the name of his God Adonai,
and they will live, for then he will be great
to the ends of the earth, and he will be peace...
and the remnant of Jacob in the midst of many peoples,
like dew from Adonai, like showers on grass,
which waits not for human beings
nor lingers for children of humanity.

RESPONSORY

The Lord has made known...
...*alleluia, alleluia.*

His saving power.

GOSPEL READING OF THE DAY (or use the **Canticle of Zechariah** from page 268)

Antiphon   Marvelous is the mystery proclaimed this day:
Luke 2:16-21   human nature is made new as God
becomes human; he remains what he was
and becomes what he was not.
Yet each nature stays distinct
and for ever undivided.

MORNING PRAYER PETITIONS AND CLOSING PRAYER, see page 269.

CHRISTMAS OCTAVE - JANUARY 1
THEOTOKOS, MARY the MOTHER of GOD
EVENING

O sanc-tis-si-ma/, O pi-is-si-ma/,
Dul-cis vir-go Ma-ri\-a!
Ma/-ter a-ma/-ta, In/ te-me-ra/-ta,
O\-ra\, O\-ra pro-no\-bis.

Ho-ly, ho-ly Ma-ry, Strong and hum-ble of Ma-ry,
Sweet-ness, vir-gin Ma-ri\-a!
Moth-er of our Sa/-vior,
       In your fi-at "yes" and more,
O\-ra\, O\-ra\, pray\ for us.

Text: *Stimmen der Volker in Liedern*, 1807
Music: 55 7 55 7, O DU FROLICHE; Tattersall's *Improved Psalmody*, 1704

PSALM 121

Antiphon
Mary, the mother of Jesus, and Joseph
were filled with wonder
at all that was said of the child.

I lift up my eyes to the hills.
From where does my help come?
My help is from and with Adonai,
Maker of heavens and earth,

who will not let your foot slip
nor slumber when watching over you.
Indeed the one watching over Israel
will not slumber and will not sleep.

Adonai watches over you,
the Most High at your right hand.
By day the sun will not harm you,
nor the moon by the night.

Adonai will keep you from all harm
and watch over your life.
Adonai will watch over your going and coming
from now and to forevermore.

Glory…

Antiphon
Mary, the mother of Jesus, and Joseph
were filled with wonder
at all that was said of the child.

PSALM 122

Antiphon
O marvelous exchange! Humanity's Creator
has become human, born of a virgin.
We have been made sharers in the divinity
of Christ who humbled himself
to share in our humanity.

I rejoiced with those saying to me,
"Let us go to Adonai's house."
Our feet stand in your gates, Jerusalem.

Jerusalem is built like a city
formed together, a compact.
There the tribes go up, the tribes of Adonai.

Make it in Israel a statute
to praise the name of Adonai,
for there the thrones stand for judgment,
thrones of the house of David.

Pray for the peace of Jerusalem!
May those who love you be secure.
May peace be within your walls,
security within your citadels.

For the sake of my sisters and brothers and friends
I will say, "Now, peace be within you."
For the sake of the house of our God Adonai
I will seek your prosperity.

Glory...

Repeat antiphon.

PSALM 127

Antiphon

By your miraculous birth of the Virgin
you have fulfilled the Scriptures:
like a gentle rain falling upon the earth
you have come to save your people.
O God, we praise you.

If Adonai does not build the house,
the builders labor in vanity.
If Adonai does not watch over the city,
the watcher stands guard in vain.

It is vanity to rise early or stay up late,
or to eat the bread of hard toil;
the Lord provides as the beloved get their sleep.
See, heritage of Adonai!

Sons are a reward, and daughters of the womb.
Like arrows in the hand of a warrior,
so are children of one's youth.

Blessed is the one whose quiver is full of them;
they will not be shamed
when they contend at the gate with enmity.

Glory…

Antiphon

By your miraculous birth of the Virgin
you have fulfilled the Scriptures:
like a gentle rain falling upon the earth
you have come to save your people.
O God, we praise you.

EPHESIANS 1:3-10

Antiphon

Your blessed and fruitful virginity
is like the bush Moses saw on Sinai, flaming
yet unburned. Pray for us, Mother of God.

Blessed be the God and Father
of our Lord Jesus Christ,
who has blessed us in Christ
with every spiritual blessing in the heavens.

God chose us in Christ
before the foundation of the world,
to be holy and free of blemish before him.

In love, God gave us a destiny:
as sons are adopted, through Jesus Christ himself,
in accord with the good pleasure of God's will
to the praise of the glory of grace
by which we are favored as God's beloved.

In Christ we have the redemption
through his blood, the forgiveness of sins,
in accord with the riches of his grace
which he made abound to us.

In all wisdom and intelligence
the mystery of God's will is made known to us
in accord with God's good pleasure and purpose:

A stewardship of the fullness of time,
heading up all things in Christ,
the things in the heavens and the things on earth.

Glory...   Repeat antiphon.

READING **GALATIANS** 4:4-5

When the fullness of time had come,
God sent forth God's own Son,
becoming of a woman, becoming under the law,
that he might redeem those under the law,
that we might receive the full adoption
as sons and daughters.

RESPONSORY Jn 1:14

The Word became flesh...
...*alleluia, alleluia.*
And dwelt among us...

GOSPEL CANTICLE (**Canticle of Mary**) see page 270.

Antiphon Blessed, O Christ,
is the womb which bore you
and the breast that nursed you,
Lord and Savior of the cosmos,
alleluia.

EVENING PRAYER INTERCESSIONS AND CLOSING PRAYER, see page 271.

CHRISTMAS MONDAY MORNINGS
Between January 1 and Baptism of the Lord

Melody: *The Glory Of These Forty Days*

The/ God whom\ earth and/ sea and sky
A-dore and laud and mag-ni-fy,
Who o'er their/ three\-fold fab\-ric reigns,
The vir-gin's spot-less womb con-tains.

The/ God whose\ will by/ moon and sun
And all things in due course is done,
Is borne up/-on\ a maid\-en's breast,
By full-est heav'-nly grace pos-sessed.

Blest/ in the\ mes-sage/ Ga-briel brought;
Blest by the work the Spir-it wrought:
The Great De/-sire\ of all\ the earth
Took hu-man flesh and hu-man birth.

All/ ho-nor\, laud, and/ glo-ry be,
To you, O Je-sus, of the Three,
All glo-ry/, as\ you ev\-er meet
Our Fa-ther and the Pa-ra-clete.

Text: Venantius Fortunatus, *Quem terra, pontus...*, d.609;
translated by John M. Neale, 1854, altered
Music option: ERHALT UNS HERR, LM; Klug's *Geistliche Lieder, 1543;*
Popular melody for: *The Glory Of These Forty Days*

MONDAY MORNINGS
(from Week II of the IV-Week Cycle)

PSALM 31:1-17,20-25

Antiphon   Lord, shine your faces on your servant, alleluia.

In you, Adonai, I take refuge;
let me not be shamed to forever.
Deliver me in your righteousness.
Quickly turn to me your ear! Rescue me!

Be for me a rock of refuge,
a fortress house to save me.
Since you are my rock and my fortress,
for the sake of your name
you lead me and guide me.

You free me from the trap they set for me,
for you are my refuge.
Into your hand I commit my spirit;
you redeem me, Adonai God of truth.

I hate when folks cling to worthless idols,
and I trust in Adonai.
I will be glad and rejoice in your love
for you saw my affliction;
you knew the anguishes of my soul.

You do not put me into the hand of enmity;
you set my feet into the spacious place.

PSALM 31, continued

Be merciful to me, Adonai, in my distress;
my eyes and my soul and my body
grow weak with sorrow.

My life is consumed by anguish
and my years with groaning.
My strength fails because of my guilt
and my bones grow weak.

Because of enmity I am
the utter contempt of even my neighbors
and a dread to my friends
who see me on the street and flee.

I am forgotten as though dead;
my heart became like broken pottery,
for I hear the slander of many
and terror on every side
when they conspire together against me
and plot to take my life.

But I trust in you, Adonai;
I say you are my God;
my times are in your hand.
Deliver me from the hands
of enmity and pursuers.

Shine your faces on your servant!
Save me in your unfailing love!...

How great is the goodness
you store up for ones who fear you
and bestow on those taking refuge in you
in the sight of the children of humanity.

You hide them in the shelter of your presence;
from human intrigues you keep them
in a dwelling safe from the strife of tongues.

Adonai is praised for showing wonderful love
to me in the city besieged, and I said in my alarm,
"I am cut off from before your eyes."
Yet you heard the sound of my cries for mercy
when I called to you for help.

Love Adonai, all you saints,
Adonai faithful and preserving,
but paying back in full the arrogant.

Be strong and strengthen your heart,
all you hoping in Adonai!

Glory...

Antiphon   Lord, shine your faces on your servant,
            alleluia.

PSALM 42

Antiphon
>When can I go
>and meet the face of God?

As a deer breathes heavy for streams of water,
so my soul throbs for you, God.

My soul she thirsts for God, the living God.
When can I go and meet the faces of God?

My tears were food for me by day and by night,
while all day they said to me, "Where is your God?"

These things I remember
as my soul pours out before me:
How I would go with the multitude
to lead them to the house of God
sounding shouts of joy and thanksgiving,
a festive throng!

Why are you downcast, my soul,
and disturbed within me?
Put hope in God, whom I will yet praise,
the saving help and presence.

My God, within me my soul she is downcast.
For this I will remember you
from the land of Jordan and the heights of Hermon,
from the Mount of Mizar:

Deep calls to deep in the roar of your waterfalls.
All your waves and breakers are swept over me.

By day Adonai directs love
and at night the song within me
is a prayer to the God of my life.

I say to El my Rock, "why do you forget me?
 Why must I go about mourning,
 oppressed by enmity?"

With mortal agony in my bones,
taunted by foes,
while all day they say to me, "Where is your God?"

Why are you downcast, my soul?
Why are you disturbed within me?
Put hope in God, whom I will yet praise,
my saving help and God.

Glory…

Antiphon   When can I go
 and meet the face of God?

SIRACH 36:1-6,13-22

Antiphon   Show mercy, Lord,
 to the people called by your name.

Come to our aid, God of all;
let all the nations be in fear of you.
Raise your hand to the foreign nations,
that they may see your might.

SIRACH 36:1-6,13-22, continued

As you have used us to show them your holiness,
so now use them to show us your glory.
They will know as we know
that there is no God but you.

Give new signs and work new wonders;
show the splendor of your right hand and arm...

Gather all the tribes of Jacob,
that they may inherit the land as at the beginning.
Show mercy to the people called by your name:
Israel, whom you named your firstborn.

Have pity on your holy city, Jerusalem,
the foundation for your throne.
Fill Zion with your majesty,
and your temple with your glory.

Give witness of your deeds of old;
fulfill the prophecies spoken in your name.
Reward those who have hoped in you,
and let your prophets be proven true.

Hear the prayers of your servants,
as you are good to your people.
Thus all will know to the ends of the earth
that you are God eternal.

Glory...

Antiphon   Show mercy, Lord,
to the people called by your name.

PSALM 19

Antiphon The heavens are declaring
the glory of God.

The heavens declare the glory of God,
and the sky proclaims the work of God's hands.
Day after day, speech pouring forth,
and knowledge on display night after night.

There is no speech, there is no language,
and no sound is heard.
Into all the earth their line goes out
and their words to the ends of the world.

There God has pitched a tent for the sun,
and like a bridegroom coming forth,
and like a champion running the course, rejoices.

At the end of the heavens is the rising,
to their furthest ends is the circuit,
and nothing is hidden from its heat.

The law of Adonai is perfect, reviving the soul;
statutes of Adonai are trustworthy,
making wise of the simple;
precepts of Adonai are right ones,
giving joy of heart;

PSALM 19, continued

the command of Adonai is radiant,
giving light to eyes;
the fear of Adonai is pure, enduring to forever;
ordinances of Adonai are sure and altogether just;

more precious than gold,
much more than pure gold,
more sweet than honey, the honey of honeycombs.

Your servant is being warned by them;
to keep them is a great reward.
Who can discern errors?
From those hidden from me, forgive me!

And keep your servant from willful sins!
May they not rule over me;
then will I be blameless
and innocent of great transgression.

May the words of my mouth be as pleasing
and the meditation of my heart be as pleasing
before you, Adonai,
my Rock and my Redeemer.

Glory…

Antiphon   The heavens are declaring
             the glory of God.

READING **ISAIAH 49:8-10**

This says Adonai:
"In time of favor, I will answer you,
and in the day of salvation I will help you.
I will keep you
and I will make you as a covenant of people
to restore land to reassign desolate inheritances,
to say to captives, 'Come out!'
and to those in darkness, 'Be free!'
They will feed beside roads,
their pasture on every barren hill;
they will not hunger, nor will they thirst,
nor will the desert heat beat on them, nor the sun.
One having compassion on them will guide them
and beside springs of waters lead them."

RESPONSORY

between January 1 and Epiphany	The Lord has made known... ...*alleluia, alleluia.* His saving power.
between Epiphany and Baptism of the Lord	All the royal powers on earth ...*will bow down in worship.* Men and women of every nation...

GOSPEL READING OF THE DAY (or use the **Canticle of Zechariah** from page 268)

between	Helpless, he lay in a manger;
January 1	glorious, he shines in the heavens.
and Epiphany	Humbled, he lives among humanity;
	eternal, he dwells with the Father.

> Jan 2 **John 1:19-28**
>
> Jan 3 **John 1:29-34**
>
> Jan 4 **John 1:35-42**
>
> Jan 5 **John 1:43-51**
>
> Jan 6 **Mark 1:7-11**
>
> Jan 7 **John 2:1-11**

between	The wise ones came from the East
Epiphany Sunday	to adore the Lord in Bethlehem.
and Baptism	Opening their treasures,
of the Lord	they offered him three precious gifts:
Matthew	gold for the great King,
4:12-17,23-25	frankincense for the true God,
	and myrrh for his burial.

MORNING PRAYER PETITIONS AND CLOSING PRAYER, see page 269.

CHRISTMAS MONDAY EVENINGS
Between January 1 and Baptism of the Lord

Melody: *Down In Adoration Falling*

In his tem-ple come be-hold him,
See the long ex-pect-ed Lord;
An-cient proph-ets had fore-told him;
God has now ful-filled this word,
Now, to praise him, Al-le-lu-ia!
Break we forth with one ac-cord.

See him in the arms of Sim-eon,
Hear the grate-ful An-na's cry;
While these a-ged saints a-dore him,
See him with the vir-gin lie.
Al-le-lu-ia! Al-le-lu-ia!
Lo, th'in-car-nate God most high.

Je-sus, who in pres-en-ta-tion
Bless-ings giv-en by your poor,
Prince and au-thor of sal-va-tion,
Seal us with your prom-ise sure,
And pre-sent us in the Spir-it
To your Fa-ther cleansed and pure.

Text: based on Luke 2:22; Henry J. Pye, d.1903, and William Cooke, d.1894, altered
Music: 87 87 87 ST. THOMAS by John F. Wade, d.1786
Popular melody for: *Down In Adoration Falling*

MONDAY EVENINGS
*(from Week **II** of the **IV**-Week Cycle)*

PSALM 12

Antiphon

Words of the Lord are flawless words,
like silver refined in a furnace of clay.

Help, Adonai, for the godly are no more;
the faithful vanish from humanity's children.
They speak the lie to each of their neighbors,
lips of flattering with heart and heart.

May Adonai close all flattering lips
and tongues speaking the boast that say:
"With our tongues we will triumph,
 our lips are with us; who is our master?"

But because of oppression of the weak,
because of groaning of needy ones,
now Adonai says, "I will arise and protect them."

Words of Adonai are flawless words,
like silver refined in the furnace of clay,
and being purified seven times over.

You, Adonai, you will keep them safe;
you are our protection to forever.
But doers of badness will still strut about
when vileness is honored among human beings.

Glory...

Repeat antiphon.

PSALM 40:2-14,17-18

Antiphon

My food is that I may do
the will of the one who sent me.

John 4:34

Waiting, I waited for Adonai,
who turned to me and heard my cry,

who lifted me from the slime pit
and from the muddy mire,
and set my feet on rock,
making firm my standing place,

and put in my mouth a new song,
a hymn of praise to our God.
Many will see and fear and trust Adonai.

Blessed is the one who trusts in Adonai
and looks not to the proud
or those turning to false "gods."

Adonai, my God, many are your deeds of wonder
and your plans cannot be equaled.
Should I speak and tell of them
they would be too many to declare.

Sacrifice and offerings you did not desire,
but my ears you pierced open for me.
Burnt offering and sin offering you did not require.
Then I said, "Here, I have come;

PSALM 40:2-14,17-18, continued

in the scroll, in the book, it is written of me.
To do your will, my God, is my desire,
and your law is within my heart."

I proclaim righteousness in the great assembly.
See my lips unsealed. You, Adonai, you know!

Your righteousness I do not hide in my heart;
your faithfulness and your salvation I speak.
I do not conceal your love and your truth
from the great assembly.

Adonai, withhold not your mercies from me,
may your love and your truth protect me always
for countless troubles surround around me.

My sins overtook me and I cannot see.
They are more than the hairs of my head
and my heart fails me.

Be pleased, Adonai, to save me;
Adonai, come quickly to help me!...

May all who seek you rejoice in you and be glad
and may lovers of your salvation say always,
"Let God be exalted."

Yet I am poor and needy.
May the Lord think of me and not delay,
my help and my deliverer, my God.

Glory...

Antiphon   My food is that I may do
            the will of the one who sent me.   John 4:34

PSALM 45

Antiphon
>You, my king,
>excel among humanity
>with anointing of grace on your lips.

My heart is stirred, a noble theme;
I recite my verses for the king;
my tongue is a pen of a skillful scribe.

You were anointed with grace on your lips,
more excellent among children of humanity.
For thus has God blessed you to forever.

Gird your sword upon your side, mighty one,
your splendor and your majesty.
Your majesty, be victorious!
Ride forth on behalf of truth and humility
and let righteousness display
awesome deeds of your right hand.

Your arrows are sharp;
let nations fall beneath you into the heart
of ones who choose enmity with the royal one
on God's throne forever and ever.
A scepter of justice is the scepter of the kingdom.

PSALM 45, continued

You love righteousness
and hate when people do bad things;
for this your God anointed you
above your companions with oil of joy,
with myrrh and aloes and cassias on your robes,
and from ivory palaces strings make you glad.

Children of royalty are honored among you
and the queen bride stands at your right hand,
honored in gold of Ophir.

Listen, daughter, and consider!
Give your ear and forget your people
and the house of your parents.
The king is enthralled for your beauty;
he is your lord, so honor him!
With the gift of your face, daughter of Tyre,
wealthy people will seek you.

The all-glorious daughter of the king is within
with interweavings of gold in her gown.
In embroidered garments she is led to the king;

her virgin companions following her
are being brought to you.
They are led in with joy and gladness;
they enter the palace of the king.

In the place of your parents will your children be,
as princes and princesses through all the land.
I will make perpetual the memory of your name
through all generations and generation.
For this the nations will praise you
ever and to forever.

Glory...

Antiphon

You, my king,
excel among humanity
with anointing of grace on your lips.

EPHESIANS 1:3-10

Antiphon   The mystery of God's will
in the fullness of time
is the heading up of all things in Christ.

Blessed be the God and Father
of our Lord Jesus Christ,
who has blessed us in Christ
with every spiritual blessing in the heavens.

God chose us in Christ
before the foundation of the world,
to be holy and free of blemish before him.

In love, God gave us a destiny:
as sons are adopted, through Jesus Christ himself,
in accord with the good pleasure of God's will
to the praise of the glory of grace
by which we are favored as God's beloved.

In Christ we have the redemption
through his blood, the forgiveness of sins,
in accord with the riches of his grace
which he made abound to us.

In all wisdom and intelligence
the mystery of God's will is made known to us
in accord with God's good pleasure and purpose:

A stewardship of the fullness of time,
heading up all things in Christ,
the things in the heavens and the things on earth.

Glory...   Repeat antiphon.

READING **COLOSSIANS 1:13-16**

The Father delivered us out of the authority of darkness
and transitioned us into the kingdom of his beloved Son
>in whom we have redemption,
>the forgiveness of our sins.
>The Son is the image of the invisible God,
>the firstborn of all creation.
>In him all things were created,
>in the heavens and on the earth,
>the visible and the invisible,
whether thrones, lordships, rulers or authorities.
All things have been created through him and for him.

RESPONSORY Jn 1:14

between	The Word became flesh…
January 1	…*alleluia, alleluia.*
and Epiphany	And dwelt among us…
between Epiphany	All people will be blessed in him…
and Baptism	…*men and women of every race.*
of the Lord	All nations will acclaim his glory…

GOSPEL CANTICLE (**Canticle of Mary**) see page 270.

between January 1 and Epiphany

> O radiant child!
> You brought healing to human life
> as you came forth
> from the womb of Mary, your mother,
> like the bridegroom
> from the marriage chamber.

between Epiphany Sunday and Baptism of the Lord

> When they saw the star
> the Magi were filled with joy;
> entering the house,
> they offered their gifts to the Lord:
> gold, frankincense and myrrh.

EVENING PRAYER INTERCESSIONS AND CLOSING PRAYER, see page 271.

CHRISTMAS TUESDAY MORNINGS
Between January 1 and Baptism of the Lord

O lit-tle town of Beth-le-hem,
    How still we/ see you lie!
A-bove a deep and dream-less sleep
    The si-lent/ stars go by;
Yet in your dark-ness shi-ning
    The ever-last-ing Light;
The hopes and fears of all the years
    Are met in you to-night.

For Christ is born of Ma\-ry,
    And fa-thered/ all a-bove,
While hu-mans sleep, the an-gels keep
    Their watch of/ won-d'ring love.
O morn-ing stars, to-geth-er
    Pro-claim the ho-ly birth
And prais-es sing to God, the King,
    And peace to all on earth.

O ho-ly Child of Beth-le-hem,
    Des-cend to/ us, we pray;
Cast out our sin and en-ter in,
    Be born in/ us to-day.
We hear the Christ-mas an-gels
    The great glad tid-ings tell:
Oh, come to us, a-bide with us,
    Our Lord Em-man-u-el!

Text: based on Micah 5:2; Phillips Brooks, 1868, altered
Music: 86 86 76 86 ST.LOUIS, Lewis Henry Redner, 1868

TUESDAY MORNING
*(from Week **II** of the **IV**-Week Cycle)*

PSALM 37

Antiphon   Wait patiently for the Lord;
the meek will inherit the land,
alleluia.

Fret not over those who do badness;
envy not those who do wrong.
For like grass their efforts will soon wither,
and like the green plant they will die away.

Trust in Adonai and do good!
Dwell in the land and enjoy safe pasture!
Delight in Adonai
who will give the desires of your heart.

Commit your way and your trust
to Adonai who will do it:
making your righteousness shine like the dawn
and your justice like the noonday sun.

Be still before Adonai and wait with patience.
Fret not over the ways of the successful,
over schemes carried out by human beings.

Refrain from anger and turn from wrath!
Fret not; it brings only evil,
for humans doing badness will be cut off,
but those who hope in Adonai will inherit the land.

A little while and bad doings will be no more;
you will look and not find them in their places.
But the meek will inherit the land
and they will enjoy greatness of peace.

Plotters of bad things to do to the righteous
gnash their teeth at them.
But the Lord laughs at them,
knowing their day is coming.

They draw their sword and they bend their bow
to bring down the poor and the needy,
to slay those of the upright way.
Their sword will pierce into their own heart
and their bows will be broken.

Better the little bit of the righteous
than the wealth of many who do bad things,
for the powers of bad doers will be broken
while Adonai upholds the righteous.

Adonai knows the days of the blameless
and their inheritance will endure to forever.
They will not wither in times of disaster
and in days of famine they will enjoy plenty.

But wicked ways will perish
and those who choose enmity with Adonai
will vanish like the beauty of fields;
like smoke they will vanish.

PSALM 37, continued

A doer of badness borrows and does not repay,
but a righteous one is generous and giving.
The blessing on the righteous is to live in the land;
the curse of doing badness is to be cut off.

The steps of human beings are made firm
by Adonai who delights in their way.
Though we stumble, we will not fall
for Adonai upholds us by the hand.

I was young and now I am old,
yet never have I seen the righteous forsaken
or their children begging bread.
Generous and lending all the day,
their children are a blessing.

Turn from evil and do good! Then live to always!
For Adonai loves the just
and will not forsake the faithful.
They will be protected to forever…
Righteous ones will inherit the land
and they will dwell in her to forever.

The mouth of the righteous he utters wisdom
and the tongue she speaks justice.
The law of their God is in their heart
and their feet do not slip.

Wicked ways lie in wait for the righteous
seeking to kill them;
Adonai will not leave them under this power
nor let them be condemned when on trial.

Wait for Adonai and keep to the way
of the one who will exalt you to possess the land,
and you will see wicked ways cut off.

I saw a ruthless human flourishing
like a native green tree,
but passing away is seen no more;
though I looked he was not to be found.

Consider the blameless and observe the upright
for the future is for the person of peace.
But sinners sinning will be destroyed together;
the future of wicked ways will be cut off.

The salvation of the righteous is from Adonai,
their stronghold in times of trouble.
Their help and deliverance and salvation,
their deliverance from ways that are wicked,
is Adonai in whom they take refuge.

Glory…

Antiphon   Wait patiently for the Lord;
the meek will inherit the land,
alleluia.

PSALM 43

Antiphon   Lord, send forth your light and your truth.

God, vindicate me;
plead my cause against a nation not godly;
rescue me from humans deceitful doing wicked.

God, my stronghold, why am I rejected?
Why must I go about mourning,
oppressed by enmity?

Send forth your light and your truth;
let them guide me to your dwellings
and bring me to your holy mountain.

Then I will go to the altar of God,
to El, my joy and delight,
and I will praise you with harp, God, my God.

Why are you downcast, my soul?
Why are you disturbed within me?
Put hope in God, whom I will yet praise,
the saving help of my face, my God.

Glory…

Antiphon   Lord, send forth your light and your truth.

ISAIAH 38:10-14,17b-20

Antiphon Lord, save us all our days.

I asked, "Must I go in the prime of my days
　through the gates of Sheol;
　must I be robbed of the rest of my years?"

I said, "I will no longer see Adonai,
　Adonai in the land of the living.
　As a dweller of the place of cessation
　I will look on humanity no longer."

My house was pulled down
and taken from me like the tent of my shepherd;
I rolled up my life,
as a weaver cuts off from a loom.

From day to night you made an end of me.
I waited till dawn;
all my bones are broken as by a lion.
From day to night you made an end of me.

Like a swift or thrush I cried;
I moaned like the dove.
My eyes to the heavens grew weak.
Lord, troubles are at me; come to my aid…

ISAIAH 38:10-14,17b-20, continued

In your love you have kept my self
out of the pit of destruction;
indeed you put behind your back all my sins.

Sheol cannot praise you
and death cannot sing to you praise,
nor can those going down the pit
hope for your faithfulness.

The living alive praise you, as I do this day.
Fathers and mothers tell the children
all about your faithfulness.

Adonai saves us;
we will play our stringed instruments
and sing in the temple of Adonai
all the days of our lives.

Glory...

Antiphon   Lord, save us all our days.

PSALM 65

Antiphon   For you, O God, silence,
and praise in Zion.

For you, O God, silence and praise in Zion,
and to you will our vow be fulfilled.

To you hearing our prayer all humanity will come.
Matters of sin overwhelmed over me;
you atoned for our transgressions.

Blessed are the ones you choose
and bring near to live in your courts.
We are filled with the goodness of your house
and the holiness of your temple.

Deeds awesome and righteous are your answer,
God of our salvation,
hope of all the ends of the earth and of the far seas.

You form mountains by your power,
arming yourself with strength.
You still the roar of the seas, the roar of their waves
and the turmoil of nations.

Those who live in far away places
fear your wonders;
in dawns of morning and in the evening
you call forth songs of joy.

PSALM 65, continued

You care for the land and water her;
with an abundance you enrich her.
God's stream is as you ordain the earth:
filled with waters, providing grain.
You drench its furrows and level its ridges;
you soften her with showers and bless the crops.

You crown the year with your bounty;
carts overflow with your abundance.
The desert grasslands are overflowing
and the hills are clothed with gladness.

The meadows are covered with the flock
and valleys are coated with grain.
They shout for joy; for joy they sing.

Glory…

Antiphon   For you, O God, silence,
and praise in Zion.

READING   **ISAIAH 62:11-12**

"See," Adonai proclaimed to the end of the earth, "Say to the Daughter of Zion, 'See your salvation coming! See his reward with him, his recompense in his company!'"
They will be called the Holy People
and the Redeemed of Adonai,
and you will be called One-Being-Sought
and the City-Not-Deserted.

TUESDAY MORNINGS - JAN 2 to BAPTISM

RESPONSORY

between January 1 and Epiphany

The Lord has made known...
...*alleluia, alleluia.*
His saving power.

between Epiphany and Baptism of the Lord

All the royal powers on earth
...*will bow down in worship.*
Men and women of every nation...

GOSPEL READING OF THE DAY (or use the **Canticle of Zechariah** from page 268)

between January 1 and Epiphany

The Word became flesh
and lived in our midst.
From his fullness we all receive
gift upon gift of his love, alleluia.

Jan 2	**John 1:19-28**
Jan 3	**John 1:29-34**
Jan 4	**John 1:35-42**
Jan 5	**John 1:43-51**
Jan 6	**Mark 1:7-11**
Jan 7	**John 2:1-11**

between Epiphany Sunday and Baptism of the Lord

The wise ones offered gifts
of gold, frankincense, and myrrh
to the Lord, the Son of God
and King Most High, alleluia.

Mark 6:34-44

MORNING PRAYER PETITIONS AND CLOSING PRAYER, see page 269.

CHRISTMAS TUESDAY EVENINGS
Between January 1 and Baptism of the Lord

A-way in a man-ger, no crib for a bed,
The lit-tle Lord Je-sus laid down his sweet head.
The stars in the sky\ looked down where he lay,
The lit-tle Lord Je-sus, a-sleep in the hay.

The cat-tle are low-ing, the Ba-by a-wakes,
But lit-tle Lord Je-sus, no cry-ing he makes;
I love you, Lord Je-sus, look down from the sky
And stay by my cra-dle till morn-ing is nigh.

Be near me, Lord Je-sus, I ask you to stay
Close by me for-ev-er, and love me, I pray;
Bless all the dear chil-dren in your ten-der care,
And fit us for heav-en to live with you there.

Text: anonymous, altered significantly
Music: 87 87 D, PLEADING SAVIOR, Joshua Leavitt, *Christian Lyre,* 1830

TUESDAY EVENINGS
(from Week II of the IV-Week Cycle)

PSALM 53

Antiphon
>When God restores
>the fortunes of the people of God,
>let Jacob rejoice, let Israel be glad.

In the heart of a fool is said, "There is no God."
The evil way is vile and corrupt;
there is no one doing good.

God looks from the heavens
on children of humanity
to see if there is one who understands,
one who is seeking God.

All of them turned away together;
they became corrupt;
there is no one doing good, not even one.

Will the ones doing evil never learn?
Devouring my people, they eat bread;
they do not call on God.

There they dreaded and dread was not there,
for God scattered the bones of attackers
put to shame in God's rejection.

Who would be brought from Zion
for the salvation of Israel?
When God restores the fortunes of God's people,
let Jacob rejoice, let Israel be glad.

Glory...

Repeat antiphon.

PSALM 54:1-6,8-9

Antiphon   See! God is helping me;
             the Lord sustains my very self.

God, save me by your name
and by your might vindicate me.
God, hear my prayer!
Listen to the words of my mouth!

For strangers attack me
and ruthless people seek my life
without regard for God before them.
See, God is helping me!
The Lord is among those sustaining my self...

With a freewill offering I will sacrifice to you;
I will praise, Adonai, your good name,
for you delivered me from all trouble
and my eye has looked
on those who would be foes.

Glory...

Antiphon   See! God is helping me;
             the Lord sustains my very self.

PSALM 49

Antiphon   You cannot serve God and mammon.
Where your treasure is
there also will your heart be.   Mt 6:24b,21

Hear this all peoples! Listen all alive in the world!
Men and women, all sons and daughters,
rich and poor alike:

My mouth will speak words of wisdom
and my heart utter the understanding of things.
I will turn an ear to a proverb;
I will expound my riddle with a harp.

Why should I fear in days of evil
the badness of deceivers who surround me,
the trusters of wealth,
and the boasters of the greatness of their riches?

No human can redeem redemption of another,
nor for oneself give a ransom to God.
Ransom of a life is costly;
no ransom is ever enough
for one to live to forever
and not see the decay.

For we see that wise people die;
like the foolish and the senseless they perish,
and leave all their wealth to others.
Their thoughts are of their houses to forever
as their dwelling for generations and generation,
and so they call lands by their own names.

PSALM 49, continued

The human, despite riches, does not endure,
but perishes just like the beasts.

This is their fate who trust in themselves
and their followers who give them approval.
Like the sheep they are destined for Sheol,
and death will feed on them too.

Upright ones will rule over them in the morning
and their form will decay in Sheol, their mansion.
But God will redeem my soul
and take me from the hand of Sheol.

Be not overawed when human beings grow rich,
when they increase the splendor of their houses.
For in death they will take none of it;
with none of their splendor will they descend.

Though during their lives they blessed themselves,
and people do praise you when you prosper,
they will go to the generation of their ancestors
and never see light to forever.

Like the beast that must perish
so is a human with riches
but still poor in understanding.

Glory...

Antiphon   You cannot serve God and mammon.
Where your treasure is
there also will your heart be.

Matthew 6:24b,21

REVELATION 4:8b,11; 5:9,10,12,13b

Antiphon Worthy is the Lamb, slain to receive
the power and riches
and wisdom and strength
and honor and glory and blessing.

Worthy are you, our Lord and our God,
to receive the glory and honor and power,
because you have created all things,
and by your will all things were created and are.

Worthy are you to receive the scroll
and to open its seals,
because you were slain
and purchased for God by your blood
from every tribe and tongue and people and nation.

You made of them to our God
a kingdom and priests,
and they will reign over the earth.

Worthy is the Lamb, slain to receive
the power and riches and wisdom and strength
and honor and glory and blessing.

Glory…

Antiphon Worthy is the Lamb, slain to receive
the power and riches
and wisdom and strength
and honor and glory and blessing.

READING **1 JOHN 1:5b-7**

God is light,
and in God there is no darkness,
none.
If we say we have communion with God
and we walk in the darkness,
we lie and are not doing the truth.
But if we walk in the light as God is in the light,
we have communion with each other,
and the blood of Jesus the Son cleanses us from all sin.

RESPONSORY Jn 1:14

between January 1 and Epiphany	The Word became flesh… …*alleluia, alleluia.* And dwelt among us…
between Epiphany and Baptism of the Lord	All people will be blessed in him… …*men and women of every race.* All nations will acclaim his glory…

GOSPEL CANTICLE (**Canticle of Mary**) see page 270.

between January 1 and Epiphany	Let us dance with delight in the Lord and let our hearts be filled with rejoicing, for eternal salvation has appeared on the earth, alleluia.
between Epiphany Sunday and Baptism of the Lord	Christ, you are Light from Light; when you appeared on earth the magi offered their gifts to you, alleluia.

EVENING PRAYER INTERCESSIONS AND CLOSING PRAYER, see page 271.

CHRISTMAS WEDNESDAY MORNINGS
Between January 1 and Baptism of the Lord

Lord, your al-migh\-ty Word
Cha-os and dark/\-ness heard, And took their flight;
Hear us we hum-bly pray,
              And where the gos-pel day
Sheds not its glo-rious ray,   Let there be light!

Sa-vior, you came\ to give
Those who in shad/\-ows live   Heal-ing and sight,
Health to the sick in mind, Sight to the in-ly blind,
Now to all hu-man-kind   Let there be light!

Spir-it of truth\ and love,
Life-giv-ing, ho/\-ly dove,   Speed forth your flight!
Move on the wa-ter's face
              Bear-ing the lamp of grace,
And in earth's sad-dest place,   Let there be light!

Ho-ly and bless\-ed Three,
Glo/-rious Trin/\-i-ty,   Wis-dom, love, might;
Bound-less as o-cean tide, Roll-ing in full-est pride,
Through the world far and wide, Let there be light!

Text: Based on Genesis 1:3, *Thou Whose Almighty Word,* John Marriott, 1813, altered

Music: 664 6664, ITALIAN HYMN (MOSCOW), Felice de Giardini, 1769

WEDNESDAY MORNINGS
*(from Week **II** of the **IV**-Week Cycle)*

PSALM 39

Antiphon

We ourselves groan in ourselves,
eagerly expecting adoption,
the redemption of our body,
alleluia.

I said, "I will watch my ways
 of sinning with my tongue;
 I will put on my mouth a muzzle
 as long as temptation is in my presence."
So in silent stillness I said nothing good,
and still my anguish increased.

My heart grew hot inside me;
in my meditation a fire burned.
I spoke with my tongue,
"Show me, Adonai, my end,
 what is the number of my days;
 let me know how fleeting I am.

See the handbreadths you made!
My days and my span are as nothing before you.
Indeed, each of all humanity stands as a breath.
Indeed, as a phantom the human goes out.
Indeed, vainly bustling about, heaping up wealth
without knowing who will get it."

PSALM 39, continued

But what am I looking for now, Lord?
My hope she is in you.
Save me from all my transgressions!
Make me not the scorn of fools.
I was silent and opened not my mouth,
for you, you have done it.

Remove your scourge from me;
from the blow of your hand I am overcome.
With a rebuke for sin you discipline the human
and you consume our wealth like a moth;
indeed we are each but a breath.

Hear my prayer, Adonai, and my cry for help;
listen, El, and be not deaf to my weeping.
For I am with you as an alien,
a stranger like all of my ancestors.
Look away from me that I may rejoice
before I depart and am no more.

Glory…

Antiphon

We ourselves groan in ourselves,
eagerly expecting adoption,
the redemption of our body,
alleluia.

PSALM 77

Antiphon
God, in your holiness way,
what "god" is as great as God?

My cry is for God, indeed I cried for help.
My cry is for God to hear me.

In the day of my distress I sought the Lord,
my hand was stretched in the night without tiring;
my soul refused to be comforted.
I remembered God and I groaned;
I mused and my spirit grew faint.

You kept open the lids of my eyes;
I was troubled and could not speak.
I thought of former days and of years long ago.
I remembered my song in the night;
my heart mused and inquired of my spirit,

"Will the Lord reject to forever,
 never to show favor again?
 Is the unfailing love vanished to forever?
 Has the promise failed for all generations?
 Has God forgotten to be merciful
 or withheld compassion in anger?"

Then I thought, "My appeal is this,
 the years at the right hand of the Most High."
I will remember the deeds of Adonai;
yes, I will remember your long-ago miracles.
I will meditate on all of your works
and consider your mighty deeds.

PSALM 77, continued

God in your holiness way,
what "god" is as great as God?
You are the God who does miracles;
you display among the peoples your power.
You redeemed your people with your arm,
the descendants of Jacob and Joseph.

The waters saw you, God,
the waters saw you and writhed;
indeed the depths were convulsed.
Clouds poured down waters,
thunder resounded in the skies,
and your arrows flashed around.

Your thunder sounded in the whirlwind,
lightnings lit up the world;
the earth trembled and quaked.
Through the sea is your path,
and your way through mighty waters,
though your footprints were not seen.

You led your people like the flock
by the hand of Moses and Aaron.

Glory...

Antiphon   God, in your holiness way,
           what "god" is as great as God?

1 SAMUEL 2:1-10

Antiphon   My heart rejoices in the Lord,
            who humbles and exalts.

My heart rejoices in Adonai,
my horn is lifted high in Adonai.

My mouth boasts over enmity,
for I delight in being delivered.
There is no Holy One like Adonai,
indeed there is no one who compares;
there is no Rock like our God.

Arrogant pride is coming from their mouth.
Do not keep talking so proudly
or proudly let arrogance come from your mouth,
for Adonai is God who knows,
by whom all deeds are weighed.

Bows of warriors are broken
but those stumbling are armed with strength.
The full hire themselves out for more food,
but the hungry ones hunger no more.
She who was barren bore seven sons;
blessed with many sons, she is pining away.

1 SAMUEL 2:1-10, continued

Adonai allows death and is making alive,
brings down to Sheol and is raising up.
Adonai allows poverty and is sending wealth,
humbling and exalting,
raising the poor from the dust
and the needy from ash-heaps
to sit with princes and inherit thrones of honor.

For Adonai's are the foundations of the earth,
setting the world upon them.
The feet of the saints will be guarded
but doers of badness will be silenced in darkness.

For not by strength does the human prevail;
Adonai shatters opposition,
thundering from the heavens.
Adonai will judge the ends of the earth,
give strength, and exalt the horn
of the one chosen and Anointed.

Glory...

Antiphon
My heart rejoices in the Lord,
who humbles and exalts.

PSALM 97

Antiphon
The Lord reigns;
let the earth be glad.

WEDNESDAY MORNINGS - JAN 2 to BAPTISM
PSALM 97

Adonai reigns; let the earth be glad.
Let all the distant shores rejoice.
Clouds and thick darkness surround the throne
founded on righteousness and justice.

Fire goes before, consuming foes on every side.
Lightnings light up the world;
the earth sees and trembles.

Mountains melt like wax before Adonai,
before the Lord of all the earth.
The heavens proclaim righteousness
and all peoples see the glory.

Let those who worship idols be shamed,
those boasting in their images.
Worship God, all you "gods."

Zion hears and rejoices
and the villages of Judah are glad
because of your judgments, Adonai.

For you, Adonai, are Most High over all the earth,
far exalted above all the "gods."

Evil is despised by lovers of Adonai,
who guards the lives of faithful ones
and delivers them from the hands of doers of bad.

Light is shed upon the righteous
and joy on the upright of heart.
Rejoice in Adonai, righteous ones,
and praise the holy name.

Glory...　　　　　　　　　　　　　　　　　Repeat antiphon.

READING   **ISAIAH 45:22-25**

"Turn to me and be saved,
all you ends of the earth,
for I am God
and there is no other.
By myself I swore integrity out of my mouth,
the word that will not be revoked.
Indeed, in front of me every knee will bow,
and every tongue will swear, and say,
'In my Adonai alone are justice and strength,'
to whom will come and be shamed
all who have raged otherwise."
In Adonai they will be found righteous
and all the descendants of Israel will exult.

RESPONSORY

between	The Lord has made known...
January 1	...*alleluia, alleluia.*
and Epiphany	His saving power.
between Epiphany	All the royal powers on earth
and Baptism	...*will bow down in worship.*
of the Lord	Men and women of every nation...

WEDNESDAY MORNINGS - JAN 2 to BAPTISM

GOSPEL READING OF THE DAY (or use the **Canticle of Zechariah** from page 268)

between January 1 and Epiphany

> Christ our God, in fullness of divinity,
> took upon himself our wounded nature,
> the new Adam, alleluia.

Jan 2 - **John 1:19-28**   Jan 4 - **John 1:35-42**   Jan 6 - **Mark 1:7-11**
Jan 3 - **John 1:29-34**   Jan 5 - **John 1:43-51**   Jan 7 - **John 2:1-11**

between Epiphany Sunday and Baptism of the Lord

> We have seen his star in the East
> and have come with gifts
> to worship the Lord.

Mark 6:45-52

MORNING PRAYER PETITIONS AND CLOSING PRAYER, see page 269.

CHRISTMAS WEDNESDAY EVENINGS
Between January 1 and Baptism of the Lord

What child is this/   who, laid to rest/
On Ma-ry's lap\ is sleep\-ing?
Whom an-gels greet/ with an-thems sweet/,
While shep\-herds watch\ are keep-ing?
This, this\ is Christ the King/,
Whom shep-herds guard\ and an-gels sing;
Haste, haste\, to bring him laud/,
The Babe\, the Son\ of Ma-ry.

Why lies he in/ such mean e-state/,
Where ox and ass\ are feed\-ing?
Good Christ-ians, fear/, for sin-ners here/
The si\-lent Word\ is plead-ing.
Nails, spear\ shall pierce him through/,
The cross be borne\ for me, for you.
Hail, hail\ the Word made flesh/,
The Babe\, the Son\ of Ma-ry.

So bring him in/-cense, gold and myrrh/,
Come peas-ant, king\ to greet\ him;
The King of kings/ sal-va-tion brings/,
Let lov\-ing hearts\ en-throne him.
Raise, raise\ a song on high/,
The vir-gin sings\ her lul-la-by.
Joy, joy\ for Christ is born/,
The Babe\, the Son\ of Ma-ry.

Text: William C. Dix, *The Manger Throne*, 1865
Music: 87 87 GREENSLEEVES with refrain, English Melody, 16th C.

WEDNESDAY EVENINGS
*(from Week **II** of the **IV**-Week Cycle)*

PSALM 52

Antiphon
        I trust in God's unfailing love
        forever and ever.

Why, mighty one, do you boast of evil
to the disgrace of El all the day?
Your tongue plots destruction
like a sharpened razor, practicing deceit.

You love evil rather than good,
falsehood rather than speaking truth.
Your tongue of deceit loves every harmful word.

Surely El will bring you down,
snatch you from your tent,
and uproot you from the land of the living.

Then the righteous will see and fear,
and they will laugh at you.
See the one who did not see God as the stronghold,
but grew strong by destruction
and trusted in the greatness of wealth.

But I am like an olive tree
flourishing in the house of God;
I trust in God's unfailing love forever and ever.

PSALM 52, continued

> I will praise you to forever for what you have done,
> and in the presence of your saints I will hope in you
> for your name is good.

Glory...

Antiphon
> I trust in God's unfailing love
> forever and ever.

PSALM 62

Antiphon
> Rest, my soul, in God alone;
> from God is my salvation

> My soul finds rest in God alone,
> from whom is my salvation,
> alone my salvation and my rock,
> my fortress never to be shaken greatly.

> Until when will you assault a human being,
> will you throw down, all of you,
> like a leaning wall or a tottering fence?

> They fully intend to topple from the lofty place;
> they delight in lies
> and bless with their mouth and curse in their heart.

> My soul finds rest in God alone,
> from whom is my hope,
> alone my salvation and my rock,
> my fortress not to be shaken.

From God is my salvation and my honor;
my mighty rock and refuge.
Trust in God at all times, people;
pour out your heart to God our refuge.

Sons and daughters of humanity are but a breath;
the so-called great ones are an illusion.
On balanced scales they both rise;
together they are only a breath.

Trust not in extortion
and take no pride in stolen things;
even when riches increase
do not set your heart on them.

One thing God has spoken,
two things I have heard:
that to God is strength and to you, Lord, is love;
and surely you will reward to each
as are our deeds.

Glory…

Antiphon   Rest, my soul, in God alone;
from God is my salvation

PSALM 67

Antiphon
May God be gracious to us,
bless us,
and shine the holy face upon us.

May God be gracious to us and bless us,
may God's faces shine upon us.
How else can your ways be known on the earth
and your salvation among all the nations?

May the peoples praise you, God,
may the peoples praise you, all of them.

May the nations be glad and sing for joy
for you rule the peoples
and guide nations of the earth into justice.

May the peoples praise you, God,
may the peoples praise you, all of them.

The land will yield her harvest, God will bless us,
and all the ends of the earth will revere our God.

Glory...

Antiphon
May God be gracious to us,
bless us,
and shine the holy face upon us.

COLOSSIANS 1:12-20

Antiphon All things have been created through him;
he is before all things
and in him all things hold together.

Give joyful thanks to the Father who made you fit
for your part of the lot of the saints in light,

who delivered us out of the authority of darkness
and transitioned us into the kingdom of the beloved Son,
in whom we have redemption, the forgiveness of our sins.

The Son is the image of the invisible God,
the firstborn of all creation.
In him all things were created,
in the heavens and on the earth,
the visible and the invisible,
whether thrones, lordships, rulers or authorities.

All things have been created through him and for him.
He is before all things,
and in him all things hold together.

He is the head of the body, the church,
and the beginning, the firstborn from the dead,
so that in all things he may hold the first place.

In him all the fullness was well pleased to dwell,
and through him reconciliation to himself of all things,
things on earth and things in the heavens,
making peace through the blood of his cross.

Glory…

Repeat antiphon.

READING **ROMANS 8:1-5**

Now there is no condemnation for the ones in Christ Jesus. For the law of the Spirit of life in Christ Jesus freed you from the law of sin and death. For the thing impossible by the law, weak through the flesh, God did, sending God's own Son in the likeness of sinful flesh condemning sin in the flesh, that the ordering of the law might be fulfilled in us, walking not in accord with the flesh but in accord with the Spirit.

RESPONSORY Jn 1:14

between	The Word became flesh…
January 1	…*alleluia, alleluia.*
and Epiphany	And dwelt among us…
between Epiphany	All people will be blessed in him…
and Baptism	…*men and women of every race.*
of the Lord	All nations will acclaim his glory…

GOSPEL CANTICLE (**Canticle of Mary**) see page 270.

between	I have come from God into the cosmos
January 1	not of myself
and Epiphany	but the Father has sent me.
between	Herod questioned the Magi:
Epiphany Sunday	What sign do you tell of a newborn king?
and Baptism	We saw a brilliant star in the heavens
of the Lord	filling the cosmos.

EVENING PRAYER INTERCESSIONS AND CLOSING PRAYER, see page 271.

CHRISTMAS THURSDAY MORNINGS
Between January 1 and Baptism of the Lord

O come, lit-tle chil-dren; come one and come all,
O come to the man-ger in Beth-le-hem's stall,
And see what our Fa-ther in heav-en a-bove
Has sent to us all on this earth with his love.

O see, in the mang-er so meek and so mild,
O see in the soft light the heav-en-ly child,
In swad-dling clothes fold-ed, his beau-ty more sweet
Than an-gels, whose voic-es his low-ly birth greet.

His bed, lit-tle chil-dren, a man-ger with hay;
His Moth-er and Jo-seph in ec-sta-sy pray,
The shep-herds in won-der their glad wor-ship bring,
While cho-rus of an-gels sweet Glo-ri-a's sing.

Text: Johann C. von Schmid, d.1854;
translated by Melanie Schute, d.1922, altered
Music: 11 11 11 11 IHR KINDERLEIN KOMMET,
by Johann A. Schulz, d.1800

THURSDAY MORNINGS
(from Week II of the IV-Week Cycle)

PSALM 44

Antiphon

> For they won victory
> not by their sword and their arm,
> but by your right hand and arm
> and the light of your faces,
> alleluia.

With our ears, God, we have heard,
our fathers told us the deed
you did in their days, in days long ago.

You drove out nations by your hand
and you planted them;
you crushed peoples and made them flourish.
For they won victory not by their sword and arm,
but by your right hand and arm
and the light of your faces, for you loved them.

You are my King and my God;
decree the victories of Jacob.
Through you we push back enmity;
through your name we trample opposition.

Indeed I trust not in my bow
and my sword does not bring me victory,
but you give to us victory over enmity
and shame the adversity.
In God we boast all the day
and we will praise your name to forever.

But you let us be rejected and humbled
and you do not go out with our armies.
You turned us back before enmity
and adversaries plundered from us.

You gave us up like sheep devoured;
among the nations you scattered us.
You sold your people for no great price,
gaining nothing from their sale.

You made us a reproach to our neighbors,
scorn and derision to those around us.
You made us a byword among the nations,
a shaking of heads among the peoples.

All the day my disgrace is before me
and my shame covers my face
at taunts of reproachers and revilers
because of avenging enmity.

PSALM 44, continued

All of this happened though we did not forget you
and were not false to your covenant.
Our hearts did not turn back
and our feet did not stray from your path,
but you pushed us into haunts of jackals
and you covered us over with deep darkness.

If we forgot the name of our God,
if we spread out our hands to a foreign "god,"
would God not have discovered this,
the One knowing the secrets of the heart?
Yet for you we face death all the day;
we are considered as sheep for slaughter.

Wake up, Lord! Why do you sleep?
Rouse yourself! Do not reject us to forever.
Why do you hide your faces
and forget our misery and oppression?

Indeed our self is brought down to the dust;
our body clings to the ground.
Rise up as our help and redeem us!
because of your unfailing love.

Glory...

Antiphon

> For they won victory
> not by their sword and their arm,
> but by your right hand and arm
> and the light of your faces,
> alleluia.

PSALM 80

Antiphon
>Shepherd of Israel,
>awaken your might;
>bring us to salvation.

Hear us, One Shepherd of Israel,
you who lead Joseph like a flock.
From your throne on the cherubim, shine forth
before Ephraim, Benjamin and Manasseh!
Awaken your might! Come to our salvation!

O God, restore us!
Make your faces shine that we may be saved!

Until when, Adonai, God of Hosts,
will you smolder against the prayer of your people?
You fed them with bread of tears
and you made them drink tears by the bowlful.
You made us a contention to our neighbors,
and enmity mocks us.

God of Hosts, restore us!
Make your faces shine that we may be saved!

Out from Egypt, you brought a vine;
you drove out the nations and you planted it.
You cleared the ground before her;
her roots took root and she filled the land.

PSALM 80, continued

Mountains were covered by her shade
and the mighty cedars by her branches.
She sent out her branches to the Sea,
and her shoots as far as the River.

Why have you broken down her walls?
All who pass by the way pick at her.
The boar from the forest ravages her,
and creatures of the field feed on her.

God of Hosts, return now!
Look down from heaven!
See and watch over this vine,
this root that your right hand planted,
and the son you raised up for yourself.
Some would burn it or cut it down;
at the rebuke of your faces may those plans perish.

Let your hand be on the one at your right hand,
the descendent of Adam you raised up for yourself.
Then we will not turn away from you;
you revive us and we will call on your name.

Adonai, God of Hosts, restore us!
Make your faces shine that we may be saved!

Glory...

Antiphon

Shepherd of Israel,
awaken your might;
bring us to salvation.

ISAIAH 12:1b-6

Antiphon
Make known among the nations
the deeds of the Lord.

I will praise you, Adonai.
Though you were angry with me,
your anger turned away and you comforted me.

Surely God is my salvation!
I will trust and will not be afraid
for Yah is my strength and my song.

Adonai became for me salvation
and you will draw with joy
waters from wells of salvation…

Give thanks to Adonai! Call on the name!
Make the deeds known among the nations!
Proclaim that the name is exalted!

Sing to Adonai, who has done glory!
Let this be known to all the world.

Shout! And sing for joy, dwellers of Zion!
For great in your midst
is the Holy One of Israel.

Glory…

Antiphon
Make known among the nations
the deeds of the Lord.

PSALM 81

Antiphon   Sing for joy
to God our strength.

Sing for joy to God our strength!
Shout to the God of Jacob!

Begin the music! Strike the tambourine,
the melodious harp and the lyre!
Sound the ram horn at the new moon,
the full moon, the day of our feast!

For this is a decree for Israel,
an ordinance of the God of Jacob,
a statute established for Joseph
when time to go out from the land of Egypt
and the language we did not understand:

"I removed the burden from their shoulders,
 their hands were freed from the basket.
 In distress you called and I rescued you;

I answered from the thundercloud
and tested you at the waters of Meribah.
Hear, my people, and I will warn you, Israel,
if you will listen to me:

 'No foreign "god" shall be among you;
 you shall bow to no alien "god."
 I am Adonai, your God,
 who brought you out of the land of Egypt.
 Open wide your mouth and I will fill it!'

But my people did not listen to my voice,
and Israel did not submit to me.
So I gave them to their stubborn heart
and they followed their devices.

If my people were listening to me,
if Israel would follow my ways,
as quickly would I subdue the enmity
and turn a firm hand to the foes.

Anyone hating Adonai would cringe
under punishment lasting to forever.
But I will feed my people with finest of wheat
and satisfy you with honey out of rock."

Glory…

Antiphon
Sing for joy
to God our strength.

READING **WISDOM 7:26-30**

Lady Wisdom Sophia is the shining of eternal light,
a spotless mirror of the working of God,
an image of God's goodness.
But one, she can do all things;
while perduring, she renews all things.
From age to age she passes into holy souls
and makes of them friends of God and prophets.

WISDOM 7:26-30, continued

God's love is as great for nothing
as for the one who lives with wisdom.
Her beauty is greater than the sun,
and every constellation of the stars.
She is superior to light itself, taken over by the night,
for evil cannot prevail against wisdom.

RESPONSORY

between January 1 and Epiphany

> The Lord has made known...
> ...*alleluia, alleluia.*
> His saving power.

between Epiphany and Baptism of the Lord

> All the royal powers on earth
> ...*will bow down in worship.*
> Men and women of every nation...

GOSPEL READING OF THE DAY (or use the **Canticle of Zechariah** from page 268)

between January 1 and Epiphany

> The Lord our God
> has come to his people
> and set us free.

> Jan 2 - **John 1:19-28** Jan 4 - **John 1:35-42** Jan 6 - **Mark 1:7-11**
> Jan 3 - **John 1:29-34** Jan 5 - **John 1:43-51** Jan 7 - **John 2:1-11**

between Epiphany Sunday and Baptism of the Lord

> Peoples will come from every place
> bearing their giftedness,
> alleluia.

Luke 4:14-22

MORNING PRAYER PETITIONS AND CLOSING PRAYER, see page 269.

CHRISTMAS THURSDAY EVENINGS
Between January 1 and Baptism of the Lord

Joy to the world, the Lord is come!
Let earth re-ceive her King;
Let ev\-'ry\ heart\\   pre-pare\ him\ room\\
And heav'n and na-ture/ sing.
And\ heav'n and na-ture/ sing.
And\ hea/v'n, and hea\\v'n and na-ture sing.

Joy to the earth, the Sa-vior reigns!
Let us their songs em-ploy,
While fields\ and\ floods\\,
   rocks, hills\, and\ plains\\
Re-peat the sound-ing/ joy.
Re\-peat the sound-ing/ joy.
Re\-peat/, Re-peat\\ the sound-ing joy.

He rules the world with truth and grace
And makes the na-tions prove
The glo\-ries\ of\\   his right\-eous\-ness\\
And won-ders of his/ love.
And\ won-ders of his/ love.
And\ won/-ders, won\\-ders of his love.

Text: based on Luke 2:10 and Psalm 98;
Isaac Watts, 1719, altered
Music: ANTIOCH CM, George Frideric Handel, 1742

THURSDAY EVENINGS
*(from Week **II** of the **IV**-Week Cycle)*

PSALM 56:2-7,9-14

Antiphon

In God I trust,
I will not be afraid;
what can humanity do to me?

Be merciful to me, my God!
Human beings pursue me all the day,
attacking with oppression
and with slander all the day.

Indeed in their pride do the many attack me.
On the day I am afraid, in you I trust.
My praise is of God's word, in God I trust.
I will not be afraid; what can a mortal do to me?

All the day they twist my words against me;
all their plots are for harm.
They conspire, they lurk, they watch my steps;
they are eager for my life…

Record my lament, put my tears in your wineskin;
are they not in your record?
Enmity will turn back on the day I call;

I will know that God is for me.
In God whose word I praise,
in Adonai whose word I praise, in God I trust.
I will not be afraid; what can a human do to me?

Upon me, God, are my vows to you;
I will present thank offerings to you
for you delivered my soul from death
and my feet from stumbling,
to walk in God's presence
in the light of the living.

Glory…

Antiphon
In God I trust,
I will not be afraid;
what can humanity do to me?

PSALM 60:3-14a

Antiphon
O God,
you burst forth upon us;
you were angry,
now restore us.

God you rejected us and burst forth upon us;
you were angry, now restore us.

You shook the land and tore her open;
mend her fractures, for she quakes!
You showed your people a desperate time;
you made us drink wine to staggering.

PSALM 60:3-14a, continued

For those who fear you, you raised a banner
to be unfurled against the bow,
that your beloved ones may be delivered.
Help us with your right hand and save us!

God spoke from the sanctuary:
"I will triumph and parcel out Shechem,
and measure out the valley of Succoth;
mine are Gilead and Manasseh,

Ephraim my head helmet, Judah my scepter,
and Moab my washbasin;
On Edom I toss my sandal
and over Philistia I shout in triumph."

Who will bring me to the Rock City?
Who will lead me to Edom?
Have you, God, not rejected us,
and not gone out, God, with our armies?

Against enmity give to us aid,
for worthless is human help.
In God will we gain the victory...

Glory...

Antiphon O God,
you burst forth upon us;
you were angry,
now restore us.

PSALM 72

Antiphon I will make you a covenant of the people,
a light for the Gentiles. Isaiah 42:6b

God, endow your justice to King Solomon
and your righteousness to the royal heir,
to judge your people in righteousness
and your afflicted with justice.

Mountains will bring prosperity to the people,
the hills too in righteousness.
He will defend people afflicted,
save the children of the needy,
and crush the oppressor.

They will fear you as long as the sun,
as long as the moon,
from generation to generations.
He will be like rain falling on a mown field,
like showers watering the earth.

In his days the righteous will flourish
in prosperous abundance til the moon is no more.
He will rule from sea to sea
and from the River to the ends of the earth.

Before him will desert tribes bow
and enmity will lick dust.
The kings of Tarshish and the distant shores
will bring tribute and present gifts,
with kings of Sheba and Seba.
They will bow down to him;
all the kings of all the nations will thus serve.

PSALM 72, continued

For he will deliver the needy one crying out
and the afflicted one when no one is helping.
He will take pity on the weak and the needy
and will save the lives of the needy ones;

he will rescue their lives
from oppression and violence,
for their lifeblood is precious in his eyes.

May he live and be given gold of Sheba,
and may all ever pray
that he be blessed all the day.

May grain be abundant throughout the land,
on tops of hills, swaying like the fruit of Lebanon,
and people flourish and thrive like grass in a field.

May his name endure to forever
and continue as long as the sun;
being thus blessed, may the nations bless him.

Praised is God, Adonai, God of Israel,
alone doing marvelous deeds.
Praised is the glory of the name to forever;
may the earth be filled with the glory of God.

Amen and amen.

Glory...

Antiphon   I will make you a covenant of the people,
a light for the Gentiles.   Isaiah 42:6b

REVELATION 11:17-18, 12:10-12a

Antiphon	Our God,
who is and who was,
has taken great power to reign.

We thank you, Lord God Almighty,
the One who is and who was;
you have taken your great power and reign.

The nations raged and your anger came,
and the time to judge the dead
and to reward your slaves and prophets,
the saints, and those fearing your name,
the small and the great...

Now have come the salvation and power
and kingdom of our God
and the authority of Christ.
The accuser of our brothers and sisters was cast,
accusing them before our God day and night.

Their victory was because of the blood of the Lamb
and by the word of their witness.
They loved their life into their death,
and so be glad, you heavens,
and all you dwelling in them.

Glory...	Repeat antiphon.

Antiphon	Our God,
who is and who was,
has taken great power to reign.

READING **1 JOHN 5:20**

We know that the Son of God has come
and has given to us discernment
that we might know the true One.
And we are in the true One
in God's Son Jesus Christ.
This is the true God and eternal life.

RESPONSORY Jn 1:14

between	The Word became flesh…
January 1	*…alleluia, alleluia.*
and Epiphany	And dwelt among us…

between Epiphany	All people will be blessed in him…
and Baptism	*…men and women of every race.*
of the Lord	All nations will acclaim his glory…

GOSPEL CANTICLE (**Canticle of Mary**) see page 270.

between	We have found Jesus of Nazareth,
January 1	the son of Joseph.
and Epiphany	He is the one
	of whom Moses and the prophets wrote.

between	The people of Seba shall come
Epiphany Sunday	bringing gold, frankincense and myrrh,
and Baptism	alleluia.
of the Lord	

EVENING PRAYER INTERCESSIONS AND CLOSING PRAYER, see page 271.

CHRISTMAS FRIDAY MORNINGS
Between January 1 and Baptism of the Lord

Of the Fa-ther's love be-got\-ten
Ere the worlds be-gan\ to be,
He is Al-pha and O-me\-ga,
He the Source, the End\-ing he,
Of the things that are, that have/\\/ been,
And that fu-ture years shall see
Ev-er-more and ev-er-more\.

This the birth for-ev-er bless\-ed
When the Vir-gin, full\ of grace
By the Ho-ly Ghost con-ceiv\-ing
Bore the Sa-vior of\ our race
And the Babe, the world's Re-deem/\\/-er,
First re-vealed his sa-cred face
Ev-er-more and ev-er-more\.

He of whom the in-spired sing\-ers
Sang of old with one\ ac-cord,
He whom voic-es of the proph\-ets
Prom-ised in their faith\-ful word:
Now he shines, the long-ex-pec/\\/-ted.
Let cre-a-tion praise its Lord
Ev-er-more and ev-er-more\.

Text: *Corde natus ex Parentis* by Aurelius C. Prudentius, 413;
translated by John M. Neal, 1854, altered
Music: 87 87 87 7 DIVINUM MYSTERIUM, 12th C. chant, Mode V

FRIDAY MORNINGS
*(from Week **II** of the **IV**-Week Cycle)*

PSALM 38

Antiphon

I confess my iniquity;
do not forsake me, Lord my salvation,
alleluia.

Adonai, rebuke me not in your anger
nor discipline me in your wrath,
for your arrows have pierced into me
and your hand has come down upon me.

There is no health in my body
because of your wrath;
my bones are unsound because of my sin.
Indeed my guilts overwhelm my head
like a heavy burden, too heavy for me.

I loathe them and they fester my wounds
because of my sinful folly.
I am bowed down and brought very low;
all the day I go about mourning.

Indeed my backside is filled with searing
and there is no health in my body.
Feeble and utterly crushed,
my heart groans in anguish.

Lord, before you is all of my longing;
my sighing is not hidden from you.
My heart pounds, my strength fails me,
and my eyes are without their light.

My friends and companions from the past
avoid being present to my woundedness,
and my neighbors stay far away.
People seeking my life set traps;
wanting to harm me, they talk of ruins
and plot deceptions all the day.

I am like a deaf man and cannot hear,
like a mute unable to open my mouth.
I became like one who does not hear,
like one whose mouth gives no reply.

Indeed, I wait for you, Adonai;
you will answer, Lord my God.
For I said, "let them not gloat over me;
  when my foot does slip, let them not exalt."

For my fall is ready for me
and my pain is ever with me.
Indeed I confess my iniquity;
I am troubled by my sin.

Vigorous ones seek enmity and for no reason,
many and numerous hating me.
Repaying the good with evil,
they slander me when I seek the good.

Forsake me not, Adonai;
my God, be not far from me.
Come quickly to my help,
Lord of my salvation.

Glory...

Antiphon I confess my iniquity;
do not forsake me, Lord my salvation,
alleluia.

PSALM 51

Antiphon A broken spirit and a contrite heart, O God,
you will not despise.

Have mercy on me, God,
in accord with your unfailing love;
in accord with the greatness of your compassion
blot out my transgressions.

Wash me of my many iniquities
and cleanse me from my sin,
for I know my transgressions
and my sin is before me always.

Against you yourself I sinned;
what I did is evil in your eyes.
You are proven right when you speak
and justified when you judge.
Surely we are sinners from birth,
from conception in a mother's womb.

Surely you desire truth in our inner parts;
in my inmost place you teach me wisdom.
You cleanse me with hyssop and I will be clean;
you wash me and I will be whiter than snow...

You let me hear joy and gladness;
let the bones you let be crushed now rejoice.
Hide your faces from my sins
and blot out all my iniquities.

PSALM 51, continued

A pure heart create in me, God!
Renew inside me a spirit to be steadfast.
Do not cast me from your presences,
nor take from me your Holy Spirit.

Restore to me the joy of your salvation
and sustain in me a willing spirit.
I will teach transgressors your ways
and sinners will turn back to you.

Save me from bloodguilt, God,
God of my salvation;
my tongue will sing of your righteousness.
Lord, open my lips
and my mouth will declare your praise.

Sacrifices give you no delight;
I could bring a burnt offering,
but it would give you no pleasure.
The sacrifices, God, you will not despise
are a broken spirit and a contrite heart.

Make Zion prosper in your pleasure,
and build up the walls of Jerusalem.
Then you will delight in the sacrifice of the just,
burnt offerings and whole offerings,
bulls offered on your altar.

Glory…

Antiphon   A broken spirit and a contrite heart, O God,
you will not despise.

HABAKKUK 3:2-4,13a,15-19

Antiphon
>Even in wrath
>you remember compassion.

Adonai, I heard your fame;
I stand in awe of your deeds, Adonai.
Now, in the midst of years, renew them!
In the midst of years, make them known!
Even in wrath you remember mercy.

Eloah came from Teman,
the Holy One from the Mount of Paran.
The heavens are covered with glory
and the earth is filled with praise

like the splendor of the rays of the sunrise
or the hand from a hiding place of power...
You came out to deliver your people,
to deliver your anointed one...

You trample on the sea,
your horses churning up the great waters.
I heard my heart and she trembled,
at the sound my lips quivered;

decay crept into my bones and my legs trembled.
Yet, I will wait patiently for the day,
calamity to come on the nation invading.

HABAKKUK 3:2-4,13a,15-19, continued

Though the fig tree does not bud
and there is no grape on the vine,
the crops of the olive fail
and fields produce no food,

the sheep cut themselves off from the pen
and there are no cattle in the stalls,
yet will I rejoice in Adonai
and be joyful in the God of my salvation.

Sovereign Adonai, my strength,
makes my feet like that of the deer,
makes me go to the heights.

Glory…

Antiphon Even in wrath
you remember compassion.

PSALM 147 :1-11

Antiphon Extol the Lord, Jerusalem!

Hallelujah! Praise Adonai!
How good it is to sing praise to our God!
How pleasant and fitting to give praise!

Adonai builds up Jerusalem,
gathers Israel's exiles,
heals the ones with broken hearts
and binds up their wounds,
determines the number of the stars,
and calls to each of them by name.

Great and mighty in power is our Lord,
with unlimited understanding.
Adonai sustains the humble
and throws wickedness to the dust.
Sing to Adonai with thanksgiving!

Make music on the harp to our God,
who covers the skies with clouds
and supplies rain to the earth,
making grass to grow on the hills,
providing food for cattle
and young ravens when they call.

Adonai finds pleasure
not in the strength of the horse
nor delight in the legs of the human,
but is delighting in those who fear Adonai
who hope in this unfailing love.

Glory…

Antiphon   Extol the Lord, Jerusalem!

READING   **ISAIAH 61:1-2a,10-11**

The Spirit of Sovereign Adonai is on me,
because Adonai anointed me
to preach good news to poor ones
and sent me to bind up ones broken of heart,
to proclaim freedom for ones being captive,
and release for ones being imprisoned,
to proclaim a year of favor of Adonai...
To delight, I delight in Adonai,
my soul rejoices in my God,
who clothed me in garments of salvation
and arrayed me in a robe of righteousness,
as a bridegroom dresses his head like a priest
and a bride adorns herself with her jewels,
for as the soil makes the sprout to come up
and as a garden makes seeds to grow
so will Sovereign Adonai make righteousness spring up
and praise before all the nations.

RESPONSORY

between	The Lord has made known...
January 1	...*alleluia, alleluia.*
and Epiphany	His saving power.
between Epiphany	All the royal powers on earth
and Baptism	...*will bow down in worship.*
of the Lord	Men and women of every nation...

FRIDAY MORNINGS - JAN 2 to BAPTISM

GOSPEL READING OF THE DAY (or use the **Canticle of Zechariah** from page 268)

between January 1 and Epiphany

He came through blood and water,
Jesus Christ our Lord.

Jan 2 - **John 1:19-28**   Jan 4 - **John 1:35-42**   Jan 6 - **Mark 1:7-11**
Jan 3 - **John 1:29-34**   Jan 5 - **John 1:43-51**   Jan 7 - **John 2:1-11**

between Epiphany Sunday and Baptism of the Lord

All who once reviled you
will come and bow in worship
before your very footprints.

Luke 5:12-16

MORNING PRAYER PETITIONS AND CLOSING PRAYER, see page 269.

CHRISTMAS FRIDAY EVENINGS
Between January 1 and Baptism of the Lord

Refrain **Go, tell it on the moun-tain,**
Over the hills and ev-'ry-where\
Go, tell it on the moun-tain,
That Je-sus Christ\ is born.

While shep-herds kept their watch-ing
O'er si-lent flocks by night
Be-hold through-out the heav-ens
There shone a ho-ly light/. *Refrain*

The shep-herds feared and trem-bled,
When lo! a-bove the earth,
Rang out the an-gels chor-us
That hailed the Sav-ior's birth/. *Refrain*

Down in a low-ly man-ger
The hum-ble Christ was born
And God sent us sal-va-tion
That bless-ed Christ-mas morn/. *Refrain*

Text: John W. Work, Jr., 1872-1925;
Folk Songs of the American Negro, Nashville, 1907
Music: 76 76 with refrain; African American Spiritual

FRIDAY EVENINGS
(from Week II of the IV-Week Cycle)

PSALM 59:2-5,10-11,17-18

Antiphon   You protect me, my God.

Deliver me from enmity;
protect me, God,
from those who rise up against me.
Deliver me from those who do evil
and save me from people of bloody ways.

See, they lie in wait for my self;
fierce people conspire against me
for no offense of me nor sin, Adonai.
For no wrong they make ready to attack;
arise to help me and look!...

For you, my Strength, I watch,
for you God, my fortress, you God are my love.

God will go before me
and gloat over ones who slander...

But I will sing of your strength
and I will sing in the morning of your love,
for you are my fortress
and my refuge in times of trouble.

To you, my Strength, I sing praise
for you God, my fortress, you God are my love.

Glory...   Repeat antiphon.

PSALM 116:1-9

Antiphon   Lord, deliver my soul from death
and my feet from stumbling.

I love Adonai
who heard my voice and my cries for mercy
and turned an ear to me,
so all during my days I will call.

Cords of death entangled me
and anguishes of Sheol came upon me;
trouble and sorrow came over me.
Then I called on the name of Adonai:
"Oh, Adonai, save my self!"

Adonai is gracious and righteous,
our God the compassionate one.
Adonai protects the simple hearted;
I was in need and then I was saved.

Return, my soul, to your rest,
for good to you has been Adonai,
who delivered my soul from death,
my eyes from tears,
and my feet from stumbling,

that I may walk before Adonai
in the land of the living.

Glory...

Antiphon   Lord, deliver my soul from death
and my feet from stumbling.

PSALM 121

Antiphon   My help is from the Lord,
                   the Maker of heavens and earth.

I lift up my eyes to the hills.
From where does my help come?
My help is from and with Adonai,
Maker of heavens and earth,

who will not let your foot slip
nor slumber when watching over you.
Indeed the one watching over Israel
will not slumber and will not sleep.

Adonai watches over you,
the Most High at your right hand.
By day the sun will not harm you,
nor the moon by the night.

Adonai will keep you from all harm
and watch over your life.
Adonai will watch over your going and coming
from now and to forevermore.

Glory…

Antiphon   My help is from the Lord,
                   the Maker of heavens and earth.

REVELATION 15:3b-4

Antiphon	King of all nations,
just and true are your ways.

Great and wonderful are your works,
Lord God Almighty.
Just and true are your ways,
King of the nations.

Who will not fear, O Lord,
or glorify your name?

Only you are holy.
All the nations will come and worship before you;
your ordinances are shown to all.

Glory...

Antiphon	King of all nations,
just and true are your ways.

READING	**ACTS 10:36-39b**

Peter said,
"You know the thing
having become throughout all Judea,
beginning from Galilee
after the baptism which John proclaimed:
Jesus the one from Nazareth,
how God anointed him
with the Holy Spirit and power.

He went about doing good
and curing all those oppressed by the diabolo.
God was with him.
And we are witnesses of all things he did,
both in the country of the Judeans
and in Jerusalem..."

RESPONSORY   Jn 1:14

between	The Word became flesh...
January 1	...*alleluia, alleluia.*
and Epiphany	And dwelt among us...

between Epiphany	All people will be blessed in him...
and Baptism	...*men and women of every race.*
of the Lord	All nations will acclaim his glory...

GOSPEL CANTICLE (**Canticle of Mary**) see page 270.

between	From heaven
January 1	the Father's voice proclaimed:
and Epiphany	You are my Son, my beloved,
	in whom I take great delight.

between	An angel warned the magi in a dream
Epiphany Sunday	to return to their country
and Baptism	by a different way.
of the Lord	

EVENING PRAYER INTERCESSIONS AND CLOSING PRAYER, see page 271.

CHRISTMAS SATURDAY MORNINGS
Between January 1 and Baptism of the Lord

Praise, my soul, the King of heav-en;
To these feet your trib-ute bring.
Ran-somed, healed, re-stored, for-giv-en,
Ev-er-more God's prais-es sing:
Al-le-lu-ia! Al-le-lu-ia!
Praise the ev-er-last-ing King.

Praise for grace and fav-or giv-en
In our an-ces-tral dis-tress.
Praise God, still the same as ev-er,
Slow to chide and swift to bless.
Al-le-lu-ia! Al-le-lu-ia!
Glo-rious love and faith-ful-ness.

As a par-ent, tend-ing, spar-ing,
Well our fee-ble frame God knows.
Gent-ly bear-ing and res-cu-ing
Us from all who'd be our foes.
Al-le-lu-ia! Al-le-lu-ia!
Wide-ly yet the mer-cy flows.

Text: from Psalm 103, Henry F. Lyte, 1834, altered
Music: 87 87 87 LAUDA ANIMA, John Goss, 1869

SATURDAY MORNING
(from Week II of the IV-Week Cycle)

PSALM 106:1-16,19-48

Antiphon

The Lord remembered the covenant for them
and relented,
alleluia.

Hallelujah! Praise Adonai!
Give thanks to Adonai who is good,
whose love is to forever.

Who can proclaim the mighty acts of Adonai?
Who can declare the fullness of praise?
Blessed are they who maintain justice,
doing the right at all times.

Remember me, Adonai, as you favor your people!
In your salvation, come with your aid for me
to enjoy the prosperity of your chosen ones,
to have joy in the joy of your nation,
and to give praise with your inheritance.

We have sinned as did our ancestors;
we have done wrong with wicked acts.
Our ancestors when in Egypt
gave no thought to your miracle deeds,
did not remember your many kindnesses,
and rebelled by *Yam Suf,* the Sea of Reeds.

PSALM 106, continued

Still you saved them for the sake of your name,
to make known your power.
You rebuked the Sea of Reeds; it dried up.
And you led them through the depths as the desert.

You saved them from the hands of foes
and redeemed them from the hand of enmity.

The waters covered the adversaries;
not one of them survived.
Then they believed in the promises made,
and sang out praise.

Soon did they forget those deeds
and would not wait for good counsel.
They craved cravings in the desert
and in the wasteland they tested their El,
who gave them their request
but sent a wasting disease on their life.

They envied Moses in the camp
and Aaron, the consecrated of Adonai…
They made a calf at Horeb
and gave worship to a cast idol.
They exchanged their Glory
for an image of a grass-eating bull.

They forgot El who had saved them,
doing great things in Egypt,
miracle deeds in the land of Ham
and awesome deeds by the Sea of Reeds.

By a word spoken they were to be destroyed,
except that Moses the chosen stood in the breach.
Then they despised the pleasant land
and did not believe the promise made.

They grumbled in their tents
and did not obey the voice of Adonai,
who lifted a hand to let them fall in the desert
and their descendents fall among the nations;
they were scattered through the lands.

They yoked themselves to Baal of Peor
and they ate of sacrifices to lifeless ones.
They provoked anger by their deeds
and a plague broke out among them.

Phinehas stood up and intervened
and the plague was checked;
this was credited to him as righteousness
for generation and generations to forever.

They angered by the waters of Meribah,
the cause of trouble for Moses,
who spoke rashly with his lips
when they rebelled against the Spirit.

They did not defeat the peoples
as Adonai commanded them,
but mingled with the nations
and adopted their customs.
They worshiped their idols
which became to them as a snare.

PSALM 106, continued

They sacrificed their sons and daughters.
They shed the innocent blood
of their own sons and daughters
whom they sacrificed to idols of Canaan,
desecrating the land by this blood.

They defiled themselves by their deeds
and prostituted themselves by their deeds.
Against the people burned the anger of Adonai,
abhorring the promised inheritance.

Into the hands of nations they were given,
ruled by their foes, oppressed by enmity,
and made subject to their power.
Many times were they delivered,
but they rebelled in their decisions
and wasted away in their sins.

On hearing their cry
the Lord took note of their distress
and remembered for them the covenant,
and relented in greatness of love.
They were made pitied by all of their captors.

Save us, Adonai our God!
Gather us from the nations
to give thanks to your holy name
and glory in your praise.

Praised be Adonai, God of Israel
from everlasting to everlasting
and let all the people say, "Amen!"
Hallelujah! Praise Adonai!

Glory…

Antiphon The Lord remembered the covenant for them
and relented,
alleluia.

PSALM 92:1-9,11,13-16

Antiphon
> It is good to proclaim
> your love in the morning
> and your fidelity at night.

It is good to praise Adonai,
to make music to your name, Most High,
to proclaim in the morning your love
and at night your faithfulness,
on the ten-string and on the lyre,
and the melody of the harp.

For you make me glad by your deeds, Adonai;
at the works of your hands I sing for joy.
How great are your works, Adonai;
very profound are your thoughts.
The senseless human does not know
and the fool does not understand.

Though wickedness springs up like grass
and doers of bad things seem to flourish,
their ways will be destroyed to forever.
But you, Adonai, are exalted to forever…

You gave me strength like a wild ox
and I was anointed with fine oil…
The just will flourish like the palm tree,
and grow like a cedar of Lebanon.

Planted in the house of Adonai,
in the courts of our God they will flourish.
In old age they will still bear fruit,
fresh and green they will stay,
to proclaim, "Adonai is upright,
in my Rock there is no wrong."

Glory…

Antiphon

It is good to proclaim
your love in the morning
and your fidelity at night.

DEUTERONOMY 32:1-12

Antiphon

Praise our God,
beyond all measure.

Listen, heavens, and I will speak:
Hear, earth, the words of my mouth.
Let my teaching fall like the rain,
let my word descend like the dew,
like showers on grass, like abundant rains on plants.

The name of Adonai I will proclaim,
and praise the greatness of our God.
The work of the Rock is perfect indeed;
all the ways of our faithful God are just
and without wrong, upright and just.

DEUTERONOMY 32, continued

The children acted corruptly with no shame,
a generation warped and crooked.
Foolish and unwise people,
you repay Adonai in this way?
Did not your Father create you
and make you and form you?

Remember the days of old!
Consider the years of generation and generation!
Ask your parents and they will tell you!
Ask your elders and they will explain to you

how the Most High gave inheritance to nations,
dividing sons and daughters of humanity
and setting up boundaries of peoples
by numbers of sons and daughters of Israel.

For the portion of Adonai is the people,
Jacob the allotment of inheritance,
found in desert land, a barren and howling waste,
shielded with care, guarded as the apple of the eye,

like an eagle stirring up the nest
and hovering over the young ones,
spreading wings to catch them
and carrying them on its flight feathers.

Led by Adonai alone,
no foreign "god" was with them.

Glory...

Antiphon Praise our God,
beyond all measure.

PSALM 8

Antiphon   Our Lord, how awesome,
how majestic is your name in all the earth.

Adonai, our Lord!
How majestic is your name in all the earth!

Your glory is set above the heavens!
From lips of children and infants
you ordained strength to bring to silence
enmity, opposition and vengeance.

When I consider your heavens,
the works of your fingers,
the moon and stars which you set in place,
what is a human that you would be mindful,
a child of Adam and Eve that you would care?

And you made us little lower than a "god"
crowning us with glory and honor,
making us to rule over works of your hands,
putting everything under our feet,

flocks and herds, all of them,
and also beasts of the field,
birds of the air and fishes of the sea,
swimming through the paths of the seas.

Adonai, our Lord!
How majestic is your name in all the earth!

Glory...

Repeat antiphon.

READING **ISAIAH 9:5-6**

A child is born to us, a son is given to us,
and the ruling will be on his shoulders.
And his name will be called Wonder-Counselor,
God of Might, Father-Everlasting, Prince of Peace.
No end to the increase of ruling and of peace,
the throne of David is established over the kingdom
to be upheld with justice and with righteousness
from now and to forever.
The zeal of Adonai Sabaoth will accomplish this.

RESPONSORY

between	The Lord has made known...
January 1	...*alleluia, alleluia.*
and Epiphany	His saving power.
between Epiphany	All the royal powers on earth
and Baptism	...*will bow down in worship.*
of the Lord	Men and women of every nation...

GOSPEL READING OF THE DAY (or use the **Canticle of Zechariah** from page 268)

between	He is the one of whom it has been written:
January 1	Christ is born in Israel,
and Epiphany	a kingdom to last forever.

Jan 2 - **John 1:19-28**   Jan 4 - **John 1:35-42**   Jan 6 - **Mark 1:7-11**
Jan 3 - **John 1:29-34**   Jan 5 - **John 1:43-51**   Jan 7 - **John 2:1-11**

between	At Cana in Galilee
Epiphany Sunday	Jesus worked the first of the signs
and Baptism	showing his glory.
of the Lord	**John 3:22-30**

MORNING PRAYER PETITIONS AND CLOSING PRAYER, see page 269.

VIGIL OF EPIPHANY
Saturday Evening

Melody: *For The Beauty Of The Earth*

Glad-ly/ **ma**-gi from of old
Did the guid-ing star be-hold;
And with/ joy they hailed its light,
Lead-ing on-ward, beam-ing bright,
So, most gra-cious Lord, may we
Ev-er-more your glo-ry see!

As with/ joy-ful steps they sped,
Sa-vior, to your hum-ble bed,
There to/ bend the knee be-fore
You whom heav'n and earth a-dore,
So may we with will-ing feet
Ev-er seek your mer-cy seat!

Ma-gi/ of-fered gifts most rare
At your cra-dle, crude and bare,
So may/ we with ho-ly joy,
Pure and free from sin's al-loy,
All our cost-liest trea-sures bring,
Christ, to you, our heav'n-ly King!

Text: from Matthew 2:1-11, William C. Dix, *As With Gladness Men of Old*, 1860, altered
Music: 77 77 77 DIX, Konrad Kocher, 1838
Popular melody for: *For The Beauty Of The Earth*

PSALM 96

Antiphon
>My own eyes have seen
>the salvation you have prepared
>in the sight of every people.

Sing to Adonai a new song!
Sing to Adonai, all the earth!
Sing to Adonai and praise the name!
Proclaim the salvation from day to day!

Declare among the nations the glory of the Lord!
Among all the peoples the marvelous deeds,
for great is Adonai, greatly being praised,
the one being feared above all so-called "gods."

For all "gods" of the nations are idols,
but Adonai made the heavens,
splendor and majesty and strength and glory
in the holy sanctuary.

Ascribe to Adonai, families of nations!
Ascribe to Adonai glory and strength!
Ascribe to Adonai the glory of the name!

Bring offerings and come into the courts!
Worship Adonai in holy splendor!
Tremble in the presence all the earth!

Say among the nations, "Adonai reigns!"
Firmly established, the world cannot be moved
and peoples will be judged with equity.

EPIPHANY - SUNDAY VIGIL (Saturday Evening)

Let the heavens rejoice and the earth be glad.
Let the sea resound and all its fullness.
Let the fields and all that is in them be jubilant,
then all the trees of the forests will sing for joy

before Adonai who comes,
who comes to judge the earth,
who will judge the world and its peoples
in justice and in truth.

Glory…

Antiphon

My own eyes have seen
the salvation you have prepared
in the sight of every people.

PSALM 97

Antiphon

Begotten of the Father
before the daystar shone or time began,
the Lord our Savior
has appeared on earth today.

Adonai reigns; let the earth be glad.
Let all the distant shores rejoice.
Clouds and thick darkness surround the throne
founded on righteousness and justice.

PSALM 97, continued

Fire goes before, consuming foes on every side.
Lightnings light up the world;
the earth sees and trembles.

Mountains melt like wax before Adonai,
before the Lord of all the earth.
The heavens proclaim righteousness
and all peoples see the glory.

Let those who worship idols be shamed,
those boasting in their images.
Worship God, all you "gods."

Zion hears and rejoices
and the villages of Judah are glad
because of your judgments, Adonai.

For you, Adonai, are Most High over all the earth,
far exalted above all the "gods."

Evil is despised by lovers of Adonai,
who guards the lives of faithful ones
and delivers them from the hands of doers of bad.

Light is shed upon the righteous
and joy on the upright of heart.
Rejoice in Adonai, righteous ones,
and praise the holy name.

Glory…

Antiphon Begotten of the Father
before the daystar shone or time began,
the Lord our Savior
has appeared on earth today.

PSALM 135

Antiphon
Great is the Lord, our God,
beyond all who are treated as "gods."

Hallelujah! Praise Adonai!
Praise the name of Adonai!
Servants of Adonai, give praise!
You who minister in the house of Adonai,
in the courts of the house of our God,

praise Adonai, for good is Adonai!
Sing praise to the Name, for it is pleasant!
Adonai has chosen Jacob, Israel the chosen treasure.

For I know that great is our Lord;
greater than all the "gods" is Adonai,
who does as Adonai pleases
in the heavens and on earth and in the deep sea,

making clouds rise from the ends of the earth,
sending lightning with the rain,
and bringing wind from the storehouses,

who struck down the firstborn of Egypt,
from human to animals,
sending signs and wonders to the midst of Egypt
against Pharaoh and against all of his servants,

having struck down many nations and mighty kings:
Sihon, king of the Amorites, and Og of Bashan,
and all the kingdoms of Canaan,
who gave their land as an inheritance,
an inheritance to Israel, the people of Adonai.

Your name, Adonai, is to forever,
your renown to generation and generation,
for you, Adonai, will vindicate your people
and will have compassion on your servants.

Idols of the nations are silver and gold,
the making of human hands.
A mouth to them but they cannot speak.
Eyes to them but they cannot see.

Ears to them but they cannot hear,
and there is no breath in their mouth.
Like them will be their makers
and all who trust in them.

House of Israel, praise Adonai!
House of Aaron, praise Adonai!
House of Levi, praise Adonai!
You who fear Adonai, praise Adonai!

Praised be Adonai from Zion,
dwelling in Jerusalem.
Hallelujah! Praise Adonai!

Glory...

Antiphon   Great is the Lord, our God,
              beyond all who are treated as "gods."

1 TIMOTHY 3:16

Antiphon
> The star burned like a flame,
> pointing the way to God, the King of kings;
> the magi saw the sign
> and brought their gifts in homage.

We confess that great
is the mystery of our fidelity:

Who was manifested in flesh,
justified in Spirit,
seen by angels,
proclaimed among nations,
believed in the world,
and taken up in glory.

We confess that great
is the mystery of our fidelity:

Glory…

Antiphon
> The star burned like a flame,
> pointing the way to God, the King of kings;
> the magi saw the sign
> and brought their gifts in homage.

READING **2 TIMOTHY 1:9-10**

God has saved us and called with a holy calling,
not according to our works
but for God's own purpose,
and given grace to us in Christ Jesus
before time eternal,
now shown through the appearance
of our Savior Jesus Christ,
ending on one hand death,
and on the other bringing to light
life and incorruption through the gospel.

RESPONSORY

All people will be blessed in him...
...men and women of every race.
All nations will acclaim his glory...

GOSPEL CANTICLE (**Canticle of Mary**) see page 270.

Antiphon Seeing the star, the magi said:
This must signify
the birth of some great king.
Let us search for him
and lay our treasures at his feet:
gold and frankincense and myrrh.

EVENING PRAYER INTERCESSIONS AND CLOSING PRAYER, see page 271.

EPIPHANY
SUNDAY MORNING

Text: from Matthew 2:1-11, John H. Hopkins, Jr., 1857, altered
Music: 88 44 6 KINGS OF ORIENT with refrain, John H. Hopkins, Jr., 1857

We three kings of O-ri-ent are;
Bear-ing gifts we tra-verse a-far,
Field and foun-tain, moor and moun\-tain,
Fol-low-ing yon-der star.

Refrain   **O** / star of won-der, star of light,
Star with roy-al beau-ty bright,
West-ward lead-ing, still pro-ceed-ing,
Guide us to your per-fect Light.

Born a King on Beth-le-hem's plain
Gold I bring to crown him a-gain,
King for-ev-er, ceas-ing nev\-er,
O-ver us all to reign.   *Refrain*

Frank-in-cense to of-fer have I;
In-cense owns a De-i-ty nigh;
Prayer and prais-ing, voic-es rais\-ing,
Wor-ship-ping God on high.   *Refrain*

Myrrh is mine, its bit-ter per-fume
Breathes a life of gath-er-ing gloom;
Sorr'w-ing, sigh-ing, bleed-ing, dy\-ing,
Sealed in the stone cold tomb.   *Refrain*

Glo-rious now be-hold him a-rise;
King and God and sac/-ri-fice;
Al-le-lu-ia! Al-le-lu\-ia!
Sounds through the earth and skies.

Refrain   **O** / star of won-der, star of light,
Star with roy-al beau-ty bright,
West-ward lead-ing, still pro-ceed-ing,
Guide us to your per-fect Light.

PSALM 72

Antiphon

Christ has appeared to us;
come, let us adore him.

God, endow your justice to King Solomon
and your righteousness to the royal heir,
to judge your people in righteousness
and your afflicted with justice.

Mountains will bring prosperity to the people,
the hills too in righteousness.
He will defend people afflicted,
save the children of the needy,
and crush the oppressor.

They will fear you as long as the sun,
as long as the moon,
from generation to generations.
He will be like rain falling on a mown field,
like showers watering the earth.

EPIPHANY - SUNDAY MORNING

In his days the righteous will flourish
in prosperous abundance til the moon is no more.
He will rule from sea to sea
and from the River to the ends of the earth.

Before him will desert tribes bow
and enmity will lick dust.
The kings of Tarshish and the distant shores
will bring tribute and present gifts,
with kings of Sheba and Seba.
They will bow down to him;
all the kings of all the nations will thus serve.

For he will deliver the needy one crying out
and the afflicted one when no one is helping.
He will take pity on the weak and the needy
and will save the lives of the needy ones;

he will rescue their lives
from oppression and violence,
for their lifeblood is precious in his eyes.

May he live and be given gold of Sheba,
and may all ever pray
that he be blessed all the day.

May grain be abundant throughout the land,
on tops of hills, swaying like the fruit of Lebanon,
and people flourish and thrive like grass in a field.

May his name endure to forever
and continue as long as the sun;
being thus blessed, may the nations bless him.

PSALM 72, continued

Praised is God, Adonai, God of Israel,
alone doing marvelous deeds.
Praised is the glory of the name to forever;
may the earth be filled with the glory of God.

Amen and amen.

Glory...

Antiphon Christ has appeared to us;
come, let us adore him.

*Psalm 63, Daniel 3, and Psalm 149, go to **Christmas Morning**, page 16*

READING **MATTHEW 2:1-12**

When Jesus was born in Bethlehem of Judea
in the days of Herod the king,
behold magi from the east arrived in Jerusalem saying,
"Where is the one born king of the Judeans?
For we saw his star in the east and came to worship him."
Now hearing this King Herod was troubled,
and all Jerusalem with him, and having assembled
the chief priests and scribes of the people
he inquired from them where the Christ was to be born.
And they told him, "In Bethlehem of Judea,
for thus it has been written through the prophet,

*And you Bethlehem, land of Judah, are not at all least
among rulers of Judah, for out of you will come forth
a ruler who will shepherd my people Israel.*
Then Herod calling the magi secretly inquired from
them carefully the time of the appearing of the star,
and sending them to Bethlehem said,
"Go and question carefully about the child,
and when you find him, report to me,
so that I also may come and worship him."
So hearing the king, they went. And behold the star,
which they saw in the east, went before them
until coming it stood over where the child was.
And seeing the star
they rejoiced with a joy great exceedingly.
And coming into the house they saw the child with
Mary his mother, and falling they worshipped him.
And opening their treasures they offered to him gifts,
gold and frankincense and myrrh.
And having been warned by a dream
not to return to Herod,
they departed by another way to their country.

RESPONSORY

All the royal powers on earth
...will bow down in worship.
Men and women of every nation...

GOSPEL CANTICLE (**Canticle of Zechariah**) see page 268.

Antiphon   The Bridegroom claims his bride;
Christ has washed away her sins
in the waters of the Jordan;
the Magi hasten with their gifts
to the royal wedding;
and the wedding guests rejoice.
Alleluia.

MORNING PRAYER PETITIONS AND CLOSING PRAYER, see page 269.

EPIPHANY
SUNDAY EVENING

Text: Traditional English Carol, 17th C., possibly 13th C.
Music: Irregular

The\ **first**/ **No**/-**el**, the/ an-gel did say,
Was to cer-tain poor shep-herds in fields as they lay;
In\ fields/ where/ they lay/ keep-ing their sheep,
On a cold win-ter's night/ that was\ so deep.

Refrain   No\-el/, No/-el, No\-el, No-el,
Born is the King/ of Is\-ra-el.

EPIPHANY - SUNDAY EVENING

They\ look/-ed/ up and/ saw\ a star
Shin-ing in\ the east/, be-yond\ them far,
And\ to/ the/ earth it/ gave\ great light,
And/ so it con-tin-ued both day\ and night.

Refrain

And\ by/ the/ light of/ that\ same star
Three/ ma\-gi came/ from coun\-try far;
To\ seek/ for a king was/ their\ in-tent,
And to fol-low the star/ wher-ev-er it went.

Refrain

This\ star/ drew/ nigh to/ the\ north-west,
O'er Beth\-le-hem/ it took\ its rest;
And\ there/ it/ did both/ stop\ and stay,
Right/ o-ver the place/ where Je\-sus lay.

Refrain

Then\ en/-tered/ in those/ ma\-gi three,
Full/ rev\-'rent-ly/ up-on\ their knee,
And\ off/-ered/ there, in his pres\\-ence,
Their/ gold\ and myrrh/ and frank\-in-cense.

Refrain

Then\ let/ us/ all with/ one\ ac-cord
Sing/ prais\-es to/ our heav\-'nly Lord;
Who\ with/ the/ Fa- ther/ we\ a-dore
And/ Spir\-it blest/ for ev\-er more.

Refrain **N**o\-el/, No/-el, No\-el, No-el,
Born is the King/ of Is\-ra-el.

PSALM 47

Antiphon

This mystery,
which has been hidden through all ages
and from all generations,
is revealed to us today.

All you nations, clap your hands!
Shout to God with cries of joy!
How awesome, Most High Adonai.

The great King over all the earth
subdued nations under us
and peoples under our feet,
and chose for us an inheritance,
the pride of Jacob the beloved.

God ascended with shouts of joy,
Adonai amid sound of trumpet.
Sing praises to God, sing praises.
Sing praises to our King, sing praises.

For God, King of all the earth, sing praises.
God reigns over the nations,
God sits on the holy throne.

Nobles of nations assemble,
the people of the God of Abraham.
God, shield of the earth, is greatly exalted.

Glory...

Repeat antiphon.

PSALM 110:1-6a,7

Antiphon

He comes in splendor,
the King who is our peace;
he is supreme over all the
kings of the earth.

Adonai said to my Lord:
"Sit at my right hand
 until I make enmity as a footstool for your feet."

A scepter of your might
Adonai will extend from Zion,
and rule in the midst of enmity!

Your troops are willing on the day of your battle.
In majesties of holiness from the womb of the dawn
to you is the dew of your youth.
Adonai swore and this mind will not change,
"You are a priest to forever
 in the order of Melchizedek."

The Lord is at your right hand
and will crush kings on the day of wrath,
will judge the nations...,
and will drink from a brook on the way
with head lifted up because of all this.

Glory...

Antiphon

He comes in splendor,
the King who is our peace;
he is supreme over all the
kings of the earth.

PSALM 112

Antiphon
A light has shone through the
darkness for the upright of heart;
the Lord is gracious, merciful and just.

Praise Adonai!
Blessed are the ones who fear Adonai,
and delight greatly in the commandments.
Mighty in the land will that one be,
and blessed with generations of upright children,

wealth and richness in their houses,
and righteousness enduring to forever.
Light dawns in the darkness
for the upright, gracious,
compassionate and righteous.

The good human, generous and lending,
conducts affairs with justice.
Surely to forever the good one will not be shaken;
remembered forever will the righteous one be.

The good will have no fear of bad news,
being steadfast of heart and trusting Adonai
with heart secure, no fear to the end,
when face to face with enmity.

The good one scatters, giving to the poor,
with righteousness enduring to forever;
the dignity of the good one will be lifted in honor.

The doers of bad things will see this and be vexed
with gnashing of teeth and a wasting away,
wicked longings coming to nothing.

Glory…

Antiphon   A light has shone through the
darkness for the upright of heart;
the Lord is gracious, merciful and just.

REVELATION 4:8b,11; 5:9,10,12,13b

Antiphon   Your blessed and fruitful virginity
is like the bush Moses saw on Sinai,
flaming yet unburned.
Pray for us, Mother of God.

Worthy are you, our Lord and our God,
to receive the glory and honor and power,
because you have created all things,
and by your will all things were created and are.

Worthy are you to receive the scroll
and to open its seals,
because you were slain
and purchased for God by your blood
from every tribe and tongue and people and nation.

You made of them to our God
a kingdom and priests,
and they will reign over the earth.

REVELATION 4:8b,11; 5:9,10,12,13b, continued

Worthy is the Lamb, slain to receive
the power and riches and wisdom and strength
and honor and glory and blessing.

Glory...

Antiphon Your blessed and fruitful virginity
is like the bush Moses saw on Sinai,
flaming yet unburned.
Pray for us, Mother of God.

READING **MATTHEW 2:19-23**

When Herod died, behold an angel of the Lord appeared
by a dream to Joseph in Egypt saying, "Rise, take the
child and his mother, and go into the land of Israel,
for the ones seeking the child's life have died."
So rising he took the child and his mother and entered
into the land of Israel. But hearing that Archelaus was
reigning over Judea instead of his father Herod, he
feared to go there, and being warned by a dream he
departed into the parts of Galilee, and coming dwelt
in a city called Nazareth, so that was fulfilled what was
spoken through the prophets, *A Nazarene he shall be called.*

RESPONSORY

All people will be blessed in him...
  ...men and women of every race.
All nations will acclaim his glory...

GOSPEL CANTICLE (**Canticle of Mary**) see page 270.

Antiphon
Three mysteries mark this holy day:
today the star leads the Magi
to the infant Christ;
today water is changed into wine
for the wedding feast;
today Christ wills to be baptized by John
in the river Jordan to bring us salvation.

EVENING PRAYER INTERCESSIONS AND CLOSING PRAYER, see page 271.

VIGIL of the BAPTISM of the LORD if on a Saturday Evening

Lord of all be-ing, thronged a-far,
Your glo-ry flames from sun and star;
Cen-ter and soul of ev-'ry sphere\\,
And yet to lov-ing hearts how near.

Sun of our life, your liv-ing ray
Sheds on our path the glow of day;
Star of our hope, your gen-tle light\\
Shall ev-er cheer the long-est night.

Lord of all life, be-low, a-bove,
Whose light is truth, whose warmth is love;
Be-fore the bril-liance of your throne\\
We ask no lus-ter of our own.

Give us your grace to make us true,
And kind-ling hearts that burn for you,
Till all your liv-ing al-tars claim\\
One ho-ly light, one heav-'nly flame.

Text: Oliver Wendell Holmes, 1809-1894
Music: JESU DULCIS MEMORIA, LM; Model 1
Popular melody for: *O Radiant Light, O Sun Divine*

PSALM 66

Antiphon
I raised you up as a light for all the nations
to proclaim my salvation
to the ends of the earth.

Shout to God all the earth!
Sing the glory of the name!
Offer glory and praise to God!
Say to God, "How awesome are you;
 how great are your deeds."

Before you and your power
those in enmity cringe.
All of the earth bow down to you,
they sing praise to you,
they sing praise to your name.

Come and see the deeds of God who is awesome,
the works on behalf of all sons and daughters.
God turned the sea into dry land;
through the river they passed on foot.

Let us rejoice in God.
God rules forever with power,
with eyes watching the nations.
Let not rebels rise up.

Peoples, praise our God! Make heard the praise!
God preserves our life among the living,
and lets not our foot to slip.

PSALM 66, continued

God, you tested us, refined us as silver is refined.
You let us be brought into prison,
you let burdens be put on our backs,
you let human beings ride over our head.

We went through the fire and through the waters
and you brought us to the place of abundance.

I will come to your temple with burnt offerings,
I will fulfill to you my vows, promised on my lips,
spoken in a time of trouble.

Sacrifices of fat animals I will sacrifice to you;
with offerings of rams I will offer bull and goats.

Come! Listen! Let me tell all who fear God
what God has done for my very self.
To God my mouth cried out
with praise on my tongue.

If I cherished sin in my heart
the Lord would not have listened.
Surely God listened and heard my voice of prayer.

God, be praised, who rejected not my prayer
nor took from within me
the Lord's own *hesed* love.

Glory…

Antiphon   I raised you up as a light for all the nations
to proclaim my salvation
to the ends of the earth.

PSALM 98

Antiphon
John was in the wilderness
baptizing and proclaiming a baptism
of repentance for the forgiveness of sins.
to preach good news to the poor.

Sing to Adonai a new song
who has done marvelous things,
working salvation at the right hand and holy arm.

Adonai made known salvation,
righteousness revealed for the eyes of the nations.
Love is remembered and faithfulness
to the house of Israel

and all the ends of the earth see
the salvation of our God.
Shout for joy to Adonai, all you earth!
Burst forth, and sing, and make music!

Make music to Adonai with harp,
with harp and the sound of singing,
with trumpets and blast of ram horn:
Shout for joy before the King Adonai!

Let the sea resound, the fullness of the world,
and those living in her.
Let the rivers clap hands,
let the mountains sing together for joy

PSALM 98, continued

before Adonai who comes to judge the earth,
who will judge the world in righteousness
and peoples with equity.

Glory…

Antiphon   John was in the wilderness
baptizing and proclaiming a baptism
of repentance for the forgiveness of sins.
to preach good news to the poor.

PSALM 135

Antiphon   I baptize you with water,
but the one who is coming
will baptize with the Holy Spirit
and with fire.   *Mark 1:8*

Hallelujah! Praise Adonai!
Praise the name of Adonai!
Servants of Adonai, give praise!
You who minister in the house of Adonai,
in the courts of the house of our God,

praise Adonai, for good is Adonai!
Sing praise to the Name, for it is pleasant!
Adonai has chosen Jacob, Israel the chosen treasure.

For I know that great is our Lord;
greater than all the "gods" is Adonai,
who does as Adonai pleases
in the heavens and on earth and in the deep sea,

making clouds rise from the ends of the earth,
sending lightning with the rain,
and bringing wind from the storehouses,

who struck down the firstborn of Egypt,
from human to animals,
sending signs and wonders into the midst of Egypt
against Pharaoh and against all of his servants,

having struck down many nations and mighty kings:
Sihon, king of the Amorites, and Og of Bashan,
and all the kingdoms of Canaan,
who gave their land as an inheritance,
an inheritance to Israel, the people of Adonai.

Your name, Adonai, is to forever,
your renown to generation and generation,
for you, Adonai, will vindicate your people
and will have compassion on your servants.

Idols of the nations are silver and gold,
the making of human hands.
A mouth to them but they cannot speak.
Eyes to them but they cannot see.

Ears to them but they cannot hear,
and there is no breath in their mouth.
Like them will be their makers
and all who trust in them.

House of Israel, praise Adonai!
House of Aaron, praise Adonai!
House of Levi, praise Adonai!
You who fear Adonai, praise Adonai!

Praised be Adonai from Zion,
dwelling in Jerusalem.
Hallelujah! Praise Adonai!

Glory…

Antiphon
I baptize you with water,
but the one who is coming
will baptize with the Holy Spirit
and with fire. *Mark 1:8*

1 TIMOTHY 3:16

Antiphon
As soon as Jesus was baptized,
he came out of the water,
and the heavens opened before him.

We confess that great
is the mystery of our fidelity:

Who was manifested in flesh,
justified in Spirit,
seen by angels,
proclaimed among nations,
believed in the world,
and taken up in glory.

BAPTISM of the LORD - VIGIL

> We confess that great
> is the mystery of our fidelity:

Glory...

Antiphon
> As soon as Jesus was baptized,
> he came out of the water,
> and the heavens opened before him.

READING **MARK 1:9-11**

> And it came to pass in those days
> Jesus came from Nazareth of Galilee
> and was baptized in the Jordan by John.
> And immediately going up out of the water
> he saw the heavens being opened
> and the Spirit as a dove coming down to him,
> and a voice out of the heavens:
> "You are my Son the beloved,
> with you I am well pleased."

RESPONSORY Luke 18:13
> Lord Jesus Christ, Son of the living God...
> ...*have mercy on us.*
> Today you revealed yourself to us...

GOSPEL CANTICLE (**Canticle of Zechariah**) see page 270.

Antiphon
> Our Savior coming to be baptized
> restores the old self to new life,
> heals our broken nature,
> and clothes us in holiness.

EVENING PRAYER INTERCESSIONS AND CLOSING PRAYER, see page 271.

THE BAPTISM OF THE LORD
SUNDAY MORNING

Songs of thank-ful-ness and praise,
Jesus, Lord, to you we raise,
Man-i-fest-ed by the star
To the ma-gi from a-far;
Branch of roy/-al Da-vid's stem
In your birth at Beth-le-hem;
Prais-es be to you ad-dressed,
God in flesh made man-i-fest.

Man-i-fest at Jor-dan's stream,
Pro-phet, Priest and King su-preme;
And as Ca-na's wed-ding guest,
In your God-head man-i-fest;
Man-i-fest/ in pow'r div-ine,
Chang-ing wa-ter in-to wine;
Prais-es be to you ad-dressed,
God in flesh made man-i-fest.

Grant us grace to see you, Lord,
Mir-rored in your ho-ly Word;
May our im-i-ta-tion show,
In your like-ness may we go;
Pure and ho/-ly may we be
At your great E-pi-pha-ny;
May we praise you, ev-er blest,
God in flesh made man-i-fest.

Text: Christopher Wordsworth, 1862, altered
Music: 77 77 D, SALZBURG; Jakob Hintze, 1678

PSALM 29

Antiphon
Come, let us worship Christ,
the beloved Son in whom
the Father was well pleased.

Ascribe to Adonai, mighty ones.
Ascribe to Adonai glory and strength.
Ascribe to Adonai the glory of the name.
Worship Adonai in holy splendor.

The voice of Adonai over the waters,
the God of glory thunders.
Adonai over mighty waters,
the voice of Adonai in power,
the voice of Adonai in majesty,
the voice of Adonai breaking cedars,

PSALM 29, continued

Adonai breaks the cedars of Lebanon
and makes Lebanon skip like a calf
and Sirion like the son of a wild ox.

The voice of Adonai strikes flashes of lightning,
the voice of Adonai shakes the desert,
Adonai shakes the desert of Kadesh.

The voice of Adonai makes the deer give birth
and strips the forests bare,
and all in the temple cry, "glory."
Adonai sits over the flood
and King Adonai is enthroned to forever.

Adonai gives strength to the people;
Adonai blesses the people with peace.

Glory...

Antiphon   Come, let us worship Christ,
                  the beloved Son in whom
                  the Father was well pleased.

Psalm 63, Daniel 3, and Psalm 149, go to **Christmas Morning**, *page* 16

READING **MATTHEW 3:13-17**

Jesus arrived from Galilee at the Jordan to John
to be baptized by him, but he forbade him saying,
"I have need to be baptized by you
and you come to me?"
But answering, Jesus said to him,
"Permit now, for thus it is fitting
for us to fulfill all righteousness."
Then he permitted him.
And having been baptized
Jesus immediately went up from the water,
and behold the heavens were opened,
and he saw the Spirit of God
coming down as a dove, coming upon him.
And behold a voice out of the heavens saying,
"This is my Son the beloved,
in whom I am well pleased."

RESPONSORY Luke 18:13

Lord Jesus Christ, Son of the living God…
…have mercy on us.
Today you revealed yourself to us…

GOSPEL CANTICLE (**Canticle of Zechariah**) see page 268.

Antiphon   Christ is baptized,
            the cosmos is sanctified,
            and he takes away our sins.

MORNING PRAYER PETITIONS AND CLOSING PRAYER, see page 269.

THE BAPTISM OF THE LORD
SUNDAY EVENING

Beau-ti-ful Sa\-vior,   King of Cre-a\-tion,
Son of\ Ma-ry\, Son of God!
Tru-ly I love\ you,   Tru-ly I'll serve\ you,
Light of my soul, my Joy, my Crown.

Fair are the mea\-dows,   Fair are the wood\-lands,
Robed in\ flow-ers of bloom-ing spring;
Je-sus is fair\-er,   Je-sus is pur\-er;
He makes our sorr'w-ing spir-it sing.

Fair is the sun\-shine,   Fair is the moon\-light,
Bright are the spark-ling\ stars on high;
Je-sus shines bright\-er,   Je-sus shines pur\-er,
Than all the an-gels in the sky.

Beau-ti-ful Sa\-vior,   Lord of the na\-tions,
Full-y\ hu-man\, full-y God!
Praise, a-do-ra\-tion,   Glo-ry and ho\-nor,
Now and for-ev-er-more be yours!

Text: based on Psalm 45:2; author unknown, 1677;
translated by Joseph A. Seiss, 1873, altered
Music: ST. ELIZABETH; Hoffman and Richter's *Schleisische Volkslieder*, 1842

PSALM 118

Antiphon   This was John's witness:
I saw the Spirit
coming from heaven
like a dove
and resting on him.

Give thanks to Adonai who is good,
whose love is to forever.

Let Israel now declare:
this love is to forever.
Let the house of Aaron declare:
this love is to forever.
Let those who fear Adonai declare:
this love is to forever.

In anguish I cried to Adonai
who answered me with freedom.
Adonai is with me, I will not be afraid.
What can any human do to me?
Before enmity I keep this in mind:
Adonai is with me, ready to help me.

Better to take refuge in Adonai
than to trust in the human;
Better to take refuge in Adonai
than to trust in a prince;

All of the nations surrounded me,
indeed did they surround me;
in the name of Adonai indeed I cut them.
They swarmed around me like bees,
they crackled like thorns in a fire;
in the name of Adonai indeed I cut them.

To push back they pushed me back to fall
but Adonai helped me.
Adonai became my strength and my song
and became to me salvation.
Shout joy and victory in your tents, you righteous.

Adonai's right hand does a mighty thing,
Adonai's right hand lifted high.
Adonai's right hand does a mighty thing.
I will not die; I will live
and proclaim these deeds indeed.
To chasten, Adonai let me be chastened,
but did not give me to death.

Open for me the gates of righteousness;
I will enter through them
and give thanks to Adonai.
This is Adonai's gate,
where righteous ones may enter.
I will give thanks to you for you answered me
and you became to me salvation.

PSALM 118, continued

The stone they rejected as builders
became the cornerstone.
With Adonai this happened
and it is marvelous in our eyes.
This is the day Adonai made;
let us rejoice and be glad.

Adonai, save now!
Adonai, grant success now!
Blessed is the one coming in the name of Adonai;
We bless you from Adonai's house.
Our El Adonai has shined light onto us.

Join with boughs the festal procession
up to the horns of the altar.
To you, my God, I will give thanks.
You, my God, I will exalt.
Give thanks to Adonai who is good,
whose love is to forever.

Glory…

Antiphon   This was John's witness:
I saw the Spirit
coming from heaven
like a dove
and resting on him.

PSALM 110:1-6a,7

Antiphon

The voice resounded from the heavens:
You are my beloved Son
with whom I am well pleased.

Adonai said to my Lord:
"Sit at my right hand
 until I make enmity as a footstool for your feet."

A scepter of your might
Adonai will extend from Zion,
and rule in the midst of enmity!

Your troops are willing on the day of your battle.
In majesties of holiness from the womb of the dawn
to you is the dew of your youth.
Adonai swore and this mind will not change,
"You are a priest to forever
 in the order of Melchizedek."

The Lord is at your right hand
and will crush kings on the day of wrath,
will judge the nations…,
and will drink from a brook on the way
with head lifted up because of all this.

Glory…

Antiphon

The voice resounded from the heavens:
You are my beloved Son
with whom I am well pleased.

PSALM 112

Antiphon

In the Jordan river
our Savior crushed the serpent's head
and wrested us free from his grasp.

Praise Adonai!
Blessed are the ones who fear Adonai,
and delight greatly in the commandments.
Mighty in the land will that one be,
and blessed with generations of upright children,

wealth and richness in their houses,
and righteousness enduring to forever.
Light dawns in the darkness
for the upright, gracious,
compassionate and righteous.

The good human, generous and lending,
conducts affairs with justice.
Surely to forever the good one will not be shaken;
remembered forever will the righteous one be.

The good will have no fear of bad news,
being steadfast of heart and trusting Adonai
with heart secure, no fear to the end,
when face to face with enmity.

The good one scatters, giving to the poor,
with righteousness enduring to forever;
the dignity of the good one will be lifted in honor.

The doers of bad things will see this and be vexed
with gnashing of teeth and a wasting away,
wicked longings coming to nothing.

Glory…

Antiphon
In the Jordan river
our Savior crushed the serpent's head
and wrested us free from his grasp.

REVELATION 4:8b,11; 5:9,10,12,13b

Antiphon
A wondrous mystery
is declared to us today:
the Creator of the universe
has washed away our sins in the Jordan.

Worthy are you, our Lord and our God,
to receive the glory and honor and power,
because you have created all things,
and by your will all things were created and are.

Worthy are you to receive the scroll
and to open its seals,
because you were slain
and purchased for God by your blood
from every tribe and tongue and people and nation.

You made of them to our God
a kingdom and priests,
and they will reign over the earth.

REVELATION 4:8b,11; 5:9,10,12,13b, continued

Worthy is the Lamb, slain to receive
the power and riches and wisdom and strength
and honor and glory and blessing.

Glory...

Antiphon   A wondrous mystery
is declared to us today:
the Creator of the universe
has washed away our sins in the Jordan.

READING   **JOHN 1:29,32,34**

John saw Jesus coming toward him and said,
"Behold,
the Lamb of God
taking the sin of the world."
And John witnessed saying,
"I beheld the Spirit
coming down as a dove out of heaven
and remaining on him...
I have seen and have witnessed
that this one is the Son of God."

RESPONSORY   Christ comes to us...
...he comes in water and in blood.
Jesus Christ is our Lord...   Jn 1:14

BAPTISM of the LORD - EVENING

GOSPEL CANTICLE (**Canticle of Mary**) see page 270.

Antiphon In his love for us
Christ Jesus poured out his blood
to wash away our sins,
and made of us a kingdom and priests
for God our Father.

EVENING PRAYER INTERCESSIONS AND CLOSING PRAYER, see page 271.

CHRISTMAS in the CALENDAR

*The Season of Christmas begins
with Evening Prayer on Christmas Eve,
the Vigil of Christmas Day.*

*Christmas Day, the Solemnity of the Nativity of the Lord,
is always December 25.*

*The Feast of the Holy Family of Jesus, Mary and Joseph
is usually on the Sunday after Christmas.*

*The Christmas Octave (8 days) concludes
on January 1, the Solemnity of Mary, the Mother of God.*

*The Solemnity of the Epiphany of the Lord
is usually on the Sunday after January 1;
in some places it is still celebrated on January 6.*

*The Feast of the Baptism of the Lord
is usually on the Sunday after Epiphany.*

*If December 25 and January 1 both fall on a Sunday,
the Feast of the Holy Family is on Friday December 30,
and the Feast of the Baptism of the Lord is on
Monday January 9, following Epiphany Sunday.*

*The Season of Christmas concludes
with Evening Prayer on the Feast of the Baptism of the Lord,
and Week 1 of Ordinary Time begins
on the following day.*

DAILY GOSPEL READINGS

(*also indicated with the antiphons for Morning Prayer*)

CHRISTMAS SEASON

December 25 is Christmas Day.
    Vigil Matthew 1:1-25
    Midnight Luke 2:1-14
    Dawn Luke 2:15-20
    Day John 1:1-18

Dec 26 Matt. 10:17-22 Stephen
Dec 27 John 20:1a,2-8 John
Dec 28 Matt. 2:13-18 The Innocents
Dec 29 Luke 2:22-35
Dec 30 Luke 2:36-40
Dec 31 John 1:1-18

Holy Family Sunday
  A Matthew 2:13-15,19-23
  B Luke 2:22-40
  C Luke 2:41-52

Mary, Mother of God
Jan 1 Luke 2:16-21

Weekdays Until Epiphany
Jan 2 John 1:19-28
Jan 3 John 1:29:34
Jan 4 John 1:35-42
Jan 5 John 1:43-51
Jan 6 Mark 1:7-11
Jan 7 John 2:1-11

Epiphany Sunday (or Jan 6)
  ABC Matthew 2:1-12

After Epiphany
  Mon Matthew 4:12-17,23-25
  Tue Mark 6:34-44
  Wed Mark 6:45-52
  Thu Luke 4:14-22
  Fri Luke 5:12-16
  Sat John 3:22-30

Baptism of the Lord
  A Matthew 3:13-17
  B Mark 1:7-11
  C Luke 3:15-16,21-22

ACKNOWLEDGEMENTS for the
HINGE HOURS MEDITAION RENDERINGS

The "hinge hours," also called *Morning Prayer* and *Evening Prayer*,
come every day, during the first hour of the day, and in the evening
near sundown or at night. For the benefit of those familiar
with the *Liturgy of the Hours,* there is a method of sort to this layout.
Many psalms from the *Office of Readings* are inserted in front of
Morning Prayer, and many psalms and canticles from *Daytime Hours* and
Night Prayer are inserted into *Evening Prayer.* Some of the repetition
of psalms and canticles in the *Liturgy of the Hours* is minimized here.

The official translation approved by the Catholic Church
for the *Liturgy of the Hours* is a beautiful translation for
chanting in monasteries and seminaries.
As a parish priest, almost all of my time with the Psalter is with the
church universal but alone with God, whether in my room, in the chapel,
or in the woods. Praying in *Lectio Divina,* trying to listen to the Lord,
I have found much prayerful fruit in several translations.

This meditation rendering follows consciously these four choices:
1. For the name *Yhvh,* or *Yahweh,* the Hebrew word **Adonai** (ah-duh-nigh')
   meaning *My Lord,* is used. In several places the words *El* or *Elyon* or
   Elohim are retrieved, as is *Sabaoth* instead of *Mighty* or *Hosts.*
2. Following the Christian understanding of one God in the three persons
   of the Trinity, masculine pronouns for God are avoided, except when
   God is referred to as Father, or in specific references to Jesus.
3. In an admittedly imperfect effort to pray the gospel as well as
   the psalms, the word *enemy* is most often rendered as *enmity.*
4. Where people are referred to as *evil,* the emphasis is shifted to
   those who *do* evil, or *ways* that are evil or bad.

There are problems with all four of these choices, and these
would be reasons to not consider this compilation in public liturgy.
Still, in my judgment, the benefits overwhelm the problems.

The primary characater of this rendering is from the grace of decades
of praying with the Psalter. May the Lord grant more of this grace.
Any errors in this rendering are entirely my own. Let us be grateful
for all those who do the real work of translating sacred scripture.

HINGE HOURS for CHRISTMAS

Again, the primary source for this work is the grace of two decades of praying the psalms, canticles and readings from several translations, including these:

The Liturgy of the Hours (Four Volumes)
Copyright © 1974 ICEL
International Committee on English in the Liturgy, Inc.

New American Bible
with Revised New Testament and Revised Psalms
Copyright © 1991, 1986, 1970 Confraternity of Christian Doctrine,
Washington, D.C. All rights reserved.
(*This is my favorite translation of the Psalms.*)

New American Bible Revised Edition (NABRE)
Copyright © 2010, 1986 Confraternity of Christian Doctrine,
Washington, D.C. All rights reserved.
(*This is the newest Catholic translation.*)

New Revised Standard Version Bible: Catholic Edition
Copyright © 1993 and 1989 by the Division of Christian Education
of the National Council of the Churches of Christ in the U.S.A.

The New Jerusalem Bible
Copyright © 1985 by Darton, Longman & Todd, Ltd. and Doubleday,
a division of Bantam Doubleday Dell Publishing Group, Inc.

The Jewish Study Bible
Copyright © 1985, 1999 by the Jewish Publication Society

The Interlinear NIV Hebrew-English Old Testament
by John R. Kohlenberger III
Copyright © 1979, 1980, 1982, 1985, 1987
by the Zondervan Corporation

The NRSV-NIV Parallel New Testament in Greek and English
by Alfred Marshall
Copyright © 1990 by the Zondervan Corporation

I am especially grateful
to all those who worked on the *New American Bible*
and to Mr. Kohlenberger and Mr. Marshall.

These other works were consulted:

The New Jerome Biblical Commentary
edited by Raymond E. Brown, S.S., Joseph A. Fitzmyer, S.J.,
and Roland E. Murphy, O.Carm.
Copyright © 1990, 1968 by Prentice-Hall, Inc.

The following volumes from the Anchor Bible:
Psalms I (1-50); Psalms II (51-100); Psalms III (101-150)
The Anchor Bible, Volumes 16, 17, and 17A
by Mitchell Dahood, S.J.
Copyright © 1965, 1966, © 1968, © 1970, Doubleday
The Wisdom of Ben Sira; The Anchor Bible, Vol. 39
by Patrick W. Skehan
Copyright © 1987, Doubleday & Company, Inc.
Tobit; The Anchor Bible, Vol. 40A
by Carey A. Moore
Copyright © 1996, Doubleday
The Wisdom of Solomon; The Anchor Bible, Vol. 43
by David Winston
Copyright © 1979, Doubleday & Company, Inc.
Daniel, Esher and Jeremiah, the Additions;
The Anchor Bible, Vol.44
by Carey A. Moore
Copyright © 1977, Doubleday & Company, Inc.

And a stack of dictionaries.

Some of the **intercessions and petitions** are drawn
from *Guadium et Spes,* "Pastoral Constitution on the Church
in the Modern World," Vatican II, 1965, paragraph 27.

Stephen Joseph Wolf
Nashville, Tennessee
www.idjc.org

Come, Holy Spirit, take hold of our lives. Sign us with your holy love.
Give us your gifts. Confirm us in faith. Spirit come.
Serafina di Giacoma, altered

PSALMS of the CHRISTMAS SEASON

Psalm 2 - page 55
Psalm 4 - page 8
Psalm 7 - pages 59, 66
Psalm 8 - page 215
Psalm 12 - page 126
Psalm 17 - page 75
Psalm 19 - page 121
Psalm 24 - page 41
Psalm 25 - page 82
Psalm 29 - page 247
Psalm 31 - page 115
Psalm 33 - page 70
Psalm 34 - page 99
Psalm 37 - page 136
Psalm 38 - page 190
Psalm 39 - page 155
Psalm 40 - page 127
Psalm 42 - page 118
Psalm 43 - page 140
Psalm 44 - page 172
Psalm 45 - page 129
Psalm 46 - page 79
Psalm 47 - pages 27, 232
Psalm 48 - page 35
Psalm 49 - page 149

Psalm 51 - page 193
Psalm 52 - page 165
Psalm 53 - page 147
Psalm 54 - page 148
Psalm 56 - page 182
Psalm 59 - page 201
Psalm 60 - page 183
Psalm 62 - page 166
Psalm 63 - page 17
Psalm 65 - page 143
Psalm 66 - page 239
Psalm 67 - pages 3, 168
Psalm 72 - pages 185, 226
Psalm 77 - page 157
Psalm 80 - page 175
Psalm 81 - page 178
Psalm 85 - page 86
Psalm 87 - page 106
Psalm 89 - page 90
Psalm 91 - page 47
Psalm 92 - page 212
Psalm 96 - pages 95, 218
Psalm 97 - pages 161, 219
Psalm 98 - page 241
Psalm 99 - page 63

Psalm 106 - page 207
Psalm 110 - pages 29, 233, 255
Psalm 112 - pages 234, 256
Psalm 113 - pages 9, 36, 101
Psalm 116 - page 202
Psalm 118 - page 252
Psalm 121 - pages 109, 203
Psalm 122 - pages 49, 110
Psalm 127 - pages 50, 111
Psalm 130 - page 30
Psalm 135 - pages 221, 242
Psalm 147 - pages 10, 37, 102, 196
Psalm 149 - page 23

CANTICLES and READINGS

OLD TESTAMENT CANTICLES

Deuteronomy 32:1-12 - 2 Sat MP, page 213
1 Samuel 2:1-10 - 2 Wed MP, 159
Sirach 36:1-6,13-22 - 2 Mon MP, 119
Isaiah 12:1b-6 - 2 Thu MP, 177
Isaiah 38:10-14,17b-20 - 2 Tue MP, 141
Daniel 3:57-90 - 1 Sun MP, 19
Habakkuk 3:2-4,13a,15-19 - 2 Fri MP, 195

NEW TESTAMENT CANTICLES

Ephesians 1 - pages 38, 51, 103, 112, 132
Philippians 2 - page 11
Colossians 1 - pages 31, 169
1 Timothy 3:16 - pages 223, 244
Revelation 4&5 - pages 151, 235, 257
Revelation 11&12 - page 187
Revelation 15 - page 204

OLD TESTAMENT READINGS

Deuteronomy 5:16 - Holy Family MP, 43
Wisdom 7:26-30 - Christmas Thu MPs, 179
Isaiah 4:2-3 - Christmas Dec 31 MP, 97
Isaiah 9:4-6 - Chris Dec 30 MP, 88
Isaiah 9:5-6 - Christmas Sat MPs, 216
Isaiah 45:22-25 - Christmas Wed MPs, 162
Isaiah 49:8-10 - Christmas Mon MPs, 123
Isaiah 61:1-2a,10-11 - Christmas Fri MP, 198
Isaiah 62:11-12 - Christmas Tue MPs, 144
Micah 5:1-4a,6 - Chris Jan 1 MP, 107

NEW TESTAMENT READINGS

Matthew 2:1-12 - Epiphany MP, page 228
Matthew 2:13-18 - Chris Dec 28 MP, 72
Matthew 2:19-23 - Holy Family Vigil, 39
                     - Epiphany EP, 236
Matthew 3:13-17 - Baptism MP, 249
Mark 1:9-11 - Baptism Vigil, 245
Luke 2:1-20 - Christmas Vigil, 12
Luke 2:22-40 - Holy Family MP, 43
Luke 2:41-52 - Holy Family EP, 52
John 1:1-18 - Christmas Day MP, 24
John 1:29,32,34 - Baptism EP, 258
Acts 4:19-20 - Chris Dec 27 MP, 64
Acts 7:54-60 - Chris Dec 26 MP, 56
Acts 10:36-39b - Christmas Fri EPs, 204
Romans 8:1-5 - Christmas Wed EPs, 170
Romans 8:3-4 - Chris Dec 27 EP, 68
2 Corinthians 8:9 - Holy Family Vigil, 39
Galatians 4:3-7 - Christmas Vigil, 12
Galatians 4:4-5 - Jan 1 Vigil, 104
Galatians 4:4-5 - Jan 1 EP, 113
Ephesians 2:3b-5 - Chris Dec 28 EP, 77
Philippians 2:6-7 - Holy Family EP, 52
Colossians 1:13-16 - Christmas Mon EP, 133
2 Timothy 1:9-10 - Epiphany Vigil EP, 224
Hebrews 1:1-2 - Chris Dec 29 MP, 80
Hebrews 1:1-4 - Christmas Day MP, 24
2 Peter 1:3-4 - Chris Dec 30 EP, 93
1 John 1:1-3 - Christmas Day EP, 32
                     - Chris Dec 29 EP, 84
1 John 1:5b-7 - Chris Dec 26 EP, 61
                     - Chris Tue EP, 152
1 John 5:20 - Christmas Thu EP, 188

SONGS for CHRISTMAS

A Mighty Fortress: 87 87 66 66 7 EIN' FESTE BURG - Christmas Dec 28 MP, page 69
Angels We Have Heard On High: 77 77 GLORIA with refrain - Christmas Eve EP, 7, 34
As Abba Loves: BUNESSAN 5554 D - Christmas Dec 27 MP, 62
Away In A Manger: 87 87 D, PLEADING SAVIOR - Christmas Dec 27 EP, 146
Beautiful Savior: ST. ELIZABETH - Baptism of the Lord Sun EP, 251
Face To Face: 87 87 87 PICARDY - Christmas Dec 30 EP, 89
Gladly Magi From Of Old: 77 77 77 DIX - Epiphany Vigil EP, 217
Go Tell It On The Mountain: 76 76 with refrain - Christmas Dec 30 EP, 200
God Our Refuge: LASST UNS ERFREUEN, LM with alleluias - Christmas Dec 27 EP, 65
God Rest Ye Merry Gentlemen: 86 86 86 with refrain GOD REST - ChristmasDec31 MP, 85
Hark A Thrilling Voice Is Sounding: 87 87 D, PLEADING SAVIOR - ChristmasJan1 MP, 105
Hark, the Herald Angels Sing: 7777777777 MENDELSSOHN - Christmas Day EP, 26
Holy Joseph, You Saluting: 87 87 D, PLEADING SAVIOR - Holy Family Sun MP, 40
How Lovely Is Your Dwelling Place: O WALY WALY, LM - Christmas Dec 29 MP, 78
In His Temple Come Behold Him: 87 87 87 ST. THOMAS - Christmas Mon EP, 125
It Came Upon The Midnight Clear: CAROL CMD - Christmas Dec 29 EP, 81
Joy To The World: ANTIOCH CM - Christmas Thu EP, 181
Lord of All Being Throned Afar: JESU DULCIS MEMORIA, LM - Baptism Vigil, 238
Lord, Your Almighty Word: 664 6664, ITALIAN HYMN - Christmas Wed MP, 154
O Come All Ye Faithful: ADESTE FIDELES - Christmas Day MP, 15
O Come Little Children: 11 11 11 11 IHR KINDERLEIN KOMMET - Christmas Thu MP, 171
O Holy Night: 11 10 11 10 11 10 11 10 10 - Holy Family Sun EP, 46
O Little Town of Bethlehem: 86 86 76 86 ST.LOUIS - Christmas Dec 28 EP, 135
O Sanctissima: 55 7 55 7, O DU FROLICHE - Christmas Jan 1 EP, 108
Of The Father's Love Begotten: 87 87 87 7 DIVINUM MYSTERIUM - Christmas Fri MP, 189
Praise My Soul the King of Heaven: 87 87 87 LAUDA ANIMA - Christmas Sat MP, 206
Silent Night: STILLE NACHT - Christmas Dec 26 EP, 58
Songs of Thankfulness and Praise: 77 77 D, SALZBURG - Baptism of the Lord Sun MP, 246
Stephen, Deacon, Protomartyr: 87 87 87 PICARDY - Christmas Dec 26 MP, 54
The First Noel: Irregular - Epiphany EP, 230
The God Whom Earth and Sea and Sky: ERHALT UNS HERR, LM - Christmas Mon MP, 114
There's a Star in the East: 10 7 11 7 with refrain - Christmas Dec 31 MP, 94
To You We Owe Our Hymn of Praise: JESU DULCIS MEMORIA, LM - Chris Dec28 EP, 74
Virgin Born, We Bow Before You: 88 7 STABAT MATER - Christmas Jan 1 Vigil EP, 98
We Three Kings of Orient Are: 88 44 6 KINGS OF ORIENT - Epiphany MP, 225
What Child Is This: 87 87 GREENSLEEVES with refrain - Christmas Wed EP, 164

Gospel Canticle For Morning
CANTICLE OF ZECHARIAH (The Benedictus)
Luke 1:68-79

✢ Blessed be the Lord the God of Israel
who chose a people,
visited them to bring redemption,

and raised salvation in the house of David,
saving strength from God's own servant,

speaking from the age of the prophets
through the mouth of the holy prophet:
Salvation out of enmity,
even out of those who hate us,

to show our ancestors how mercy works,
and to remember the holy promise of the Lord,

the covenant made for our father Abraham,
calming our fear and making us free
to serve God as holy and righteous and just
in the Lord's presence all our days.

And you also child
will be called a prophet of the Most High
for you will go before the Lord to prepare his way

and give to his people a knowledge of salvation
known in accepting forgiveness of their sins.

From the deepness of God's mercy on us,
a sun rising from the height will visit to appear
to those who sit in the dark or shadow of death,
and to guide our feet into the way of peace.

Traditional Doxology

> *Glory to the Father and to the Son*
> *and to the Holy Spirit,*
> *As it was in the beginning, is now,*
> *and will be forever. Amen.*

MORNING PRAYER PETITIONS FOR THE CONSECRATION TO GOD OF THE DAY AND ITS WORK

For the Church and her ministry and apostolates…
For secular authorities and all serving as stewards…
For people who are poor or sick or in sorrow…
For respect for the dignity of each human person…
For any elders or children who feel abandoned…
For the respect due migrant workers and refugees…
For starving people awakening our consciences…
For people living in subhuman conditions…
For human beings who are enslaved or tortured…
For workers in degrading or unsafe conditions…
For peace and the basic needs of each family…
For consensus on both rights and responsibilities…
For loving respect for folks who think differently…
For the world peace that only God can give…
For a culture of vocations all over the world…
In gratitude for blessings and grace…
For those who have asked for my prayer…
For those for whom I have promised to pray…
For those who weigh on my heart…

CLOSING PRAYER

Our Fa-ther…

Gospel Canticle For Evening
CANTICLE OF MARY (The Magnificat)
Luke 1:46-55

✢ My soul is stretched full with praise of the Lord,
and my spirit, beyond joy in God, my Savior,
who chose to lay eyes on this humble servant.

Behold, now and forward,
each and every age will call me blessed,
for the Mighty One did great things to me.

Holy is the name and the mercy
to generations and generations,
the ones fearing the One,

Who scattered the haughty of mind and heart,
pulled the powerful off their high place,
and lifted with dignity the humble in need.

The hungering are filled with good things,
the rich are sent away empty,
and servant Israel is given relief

with a memory of mercy to remember,
the promise spoken to our ancestors,
to Abraham and his descendants forever.

Traditional Doxology

Glory to the Father and to the Son
and to the Holy Spirit,
As it was in the beginning, is now,
and will be forever. Amen.

HINGE HOURS for ADVENT & CHRISTMAS

EVENING PRAYER INTERCESSIONS

In gratitude for blessings, Abba thank you…
For the sins of this day, Lord Jesus have mercy…
With concerns over tomorrow, Holy Spirit help…
For faithful renewal of the Church…
For Pope N. and our Bishops…
For unity in our diversity…
For loving fidelity for all married couples…
For growth of our youth in wisdom and grace…
For workers in all the vineyards of the Lord…
For the inspiration of mercy-justice for all leaders…
For assistance for those in need…
For consoling presence for all who suffer…
For those who have died and those who grieve…

CLOSING PRAYER

Our Fa-ther,
who art in heav-en,
hal-lowed be thy name.
Thy king-dom come,
thy will be done
on earth as it is in heav-en.
Give us this day our dai-ly bread
and for-give us our tres-pass-es,
as we for-give those who tres-pass a-gainst\ us,
and lead us not in-to temp-ta/-tion,
but de-liv-er us from e\-vil.
A-men.

www.ingramcontent.com/pod-product-compliance
Lightning Source LLC
Chambersburg PA
CBHW030311080526
44584CB00012B/521